AWAKEN

Your Miracle
FREQUENCY

IT'S EASIER THAN YOU THINK TO HAVE IT ALL

by Clare Emily Williamson

Edited by Lil Barcaski and Linda Hinkle

Published by: GWN Publishing
www.GWNPublishing.com

Cover Design: Kristina Conatser

Paperback ISBN: 978-1-959608-27-1

E-Book ISBN: 978-1-959608-28-8

DEDICATION

Dad, if you read this, I love you. And you, too, Mum. I love you both more than I have the words to say. Thank you for all you have contributed to my life.

TABLE OF CONTENTS

SECTION 3:
THE "HOW"

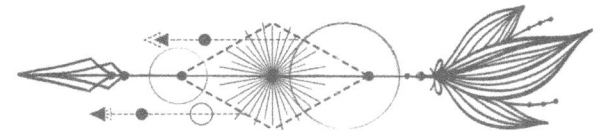

FOREWORD

Clare showed up to our reality show, Play To Win, with a twinkle in her eye and boundless energy. No small feat after having travelled 28 hours from New Zealand to Florida. I'm the Member Success Manager for Higdon Group, a Fortune 5000 coaching and training company for leaders in the network marketing industry, and I served as one of the judges during the competition.

After hearing Clare's story, I was filled with admiration at her strength and determination to rise above a horrendous, life-threatening episode that caught her unawares. Her victory over physical and emotional trauma and financial devastation is a story of true grit that challenges each one of us to greater heights.

A good coach is someone who has self-awareness, a genuine desire to help others succeed, and instinctively knows how to approach different situations. I believe a great coach is one who overcomes adversity and is vulnerable enough to share her experiences to help others break through the blocks to their success.

In *Awaken Your Miracle Frequency; It's Easier Than You Think To Have It All*, Clare steps out masterfully to help you uncover and overcome the challenges you face, and her insights become your gift. Whether you are at an impasse today and long to move forward, or are simply in a holding pattern, the choice is yours. Unwrap the gift. Let this book speak to your heart and move you to embrace the life you long to live and the success that awaits you.

MARY KATE O'CONNELL
Member Success Manager
Higdon Group

"Look to this day

For it is life,

The very life of life.

In its brief course lie all

The realities and verities of existence.

The bliss of growth,

The splendour of action,

The glory of power -

For yesterday is but a dream

And tomorrow is only a vision.

But today, well lived

Makes every yesterday a dream of happiness

And every tomorrow, a vision of hope.

Look well therefore, to this day."

SANSKRIT PROVERB BY KALIDASA, Indian poet and playwright, 4th century A.D.

Clare... the concept you have will create a collective consciousness... the world needs this.

To those of you about to embark on this journey with her, I say in Te Reo Maori (the language of the indigenous people of New Zealand), Kia kaha, kia mia, kia manawanui which translates as Be Strong, Be Steadfast, Be Willing.

MARJ FOX

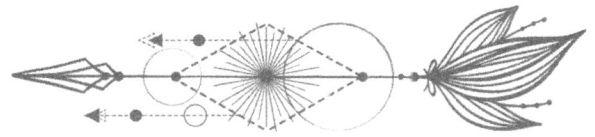

INTRODUCTION

"In order to grow, we have to break."
CLARE WILLIAMSON

*T*his is the unwritten rule of expansion. Only we fight breaking. We hold on. We try to survive. We resist change. Our resistance comes from the pain of our past experiences. And so, we unconsciously develop self-defeating patterns that mean we will never unleash the millionaire we feel inside.

In this book, I open myself wide to you about my own past and how it left me broken to what I feared was beyond repair. That is, until I rediscovered my creative power, found true flow, stopped surviving and started manifesting the life of my dreams.

I deciphered my **Abundance Code**.

I broke through my limiting beliefs and paradigms and let go of fear.

The limiting paradigm that things are scarce encourages the culture of holding on, trying to control and force things entrenched within our society, and this is making us work harder than we need to for what we want.

You *can* have it all and it *can* be EASY.

In this book, I will teach you:

- How to stop placing limits on yourself and questioning what your heart draws you to.
- How to listen to your heart and live out your true Soul Goal.
- How to live in wild abundance.

Abundance equals choice and choice equals freedom.

Freedom is my #1 value in life, only I wasn't free for so many years of my life because I was trapped by my own limiting beliefs, which were born out of experiences that had created too much fear and caution. I played small and was misaligned to my Soul Goal.

Then, I changed EVERYTHING. I went from unconsciously creating a life that kept me safe from everything I feared to consciously creating a life of abundance, with me and my power at its source.

If you are ready to unleash your "Inner Millionaire," the powerful and impactful version of yourself and if you feel the call to create positive change in the world, but know you are playing small, then this book will give you the deep epiphany you need about your own potential, so you can go from an unconscious victim to a powerful creator of your own reality.

You will see how you have attracted every experience you have had into your life and how your past is your greatest power you have to create the future you want.

This will change the game for you if your income, impact or even life experience is plateaued right now.

You will finally understand why you feel so blocked in putting yourself into the bold action that will change things and realise your dreams. And you will learn the practical steps to break through your limiting beliefs and emotions.

This book will be your guide and a tool on how to heal, release, grow, and believe that the impossible really is possible, whatever your circumstances have been in life. You will understand how to tap into the **Quantum Field** through a higher consciousness that will literally save the world and fully embrace the vulnerability of everything you fear about living out your deepest potential. You will find your wings and begin to fly on the current of your dreams, full of joy, happiness and a ripple effect of healing that washes over the world through your impact.

DISCLAIMER: Nothing in this book should be taken as financial, medical or other advice, or a guarantee of results. This book is a tool to help you awaken your **Miracle Frequency**, so that you can have it all easily. This requires your participation. The Practical Integrations throughout this book coach you to take the steps indicated to decipher your **Abundance Code** and unleash your **Inner Millionaire.**

SECTION 1

YOUR UNLEASHED VISION

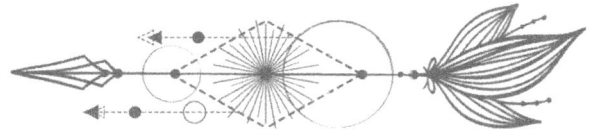

HOW TO UNLEASH YOUR
INNER MILLIONAIRE

"Truth sets us free."
JIM ROHN

*T*he start of any change comes from acknowledging that change is needed. Oftentimes, we stay stuck in life for many years simply because "stuck" is familiar. The brain favours familiarity and will work hard to make sure your familiar reality repeats itself. This might look like repeatedly finding yourself in jobs or relationships where you are undervalued, are broke, or making money and then losing it again.

When I was 8 years old, I would regularly climb the tree in our garden. My mum warned me frequently that I would fall from it. She would watch my brother and I playing from the kitchen window while she washed up, or puttered around preparing lunch, and as soon as she looked away, we'd be up the tree climbing to our heart's content, feeling the freedom of the height of the branches and not really fearing the fall at all. Why would we? We hadn't fallen yet.

One day, my foot slipped, and I went tumbling off the branch and landed legs akimbo over the frame of my bicycle parked below. I screamed so loud my mum came running full pelt down the garden, cursing that she'd told me about "climbing that tree." She reminded me of every reason why I shouldn't have climbed it and how she knew I'd end up injured like this, or worse, and how I was lucky nothing was broken.

My vagina felt like it was broken though. It throbbed for days. I had to use ice packs to sit down, and it hurt to pee. I thought twice the next time I stood at the foot of a tree whose twisted branches and enticing height beckoned me up to explore it. I'd been hurt by that experience, and my brain was smart. It wasn't going to let me make that mistake again.

"LIFE THROUGH A LENS"

That was the original title of this book from the idea that the lens through which we view our world guides the decisions we make, which in turn decides our fate. Our past experiences "frame" our beliefs and so, dictate our present and future actions.

When we are very young, there is no lens. Only our big, wide eyes looking out on a world of pure opportunity. Then one thing happens that makes us more cautious, then another thing happens that makes us more conscious still, and the lens gets narrower. We become bound by our own limiting beliefs and behaviours, until we wind up ...

Where?

I can tell you what happened to me.

I decided insignificance was safer than standing out and that playing small was safer than levelling up. I shut down my voice and my self-expression. I developed chronic anxiety, and I unconsciously chose to collapse into a world created by the belief that I was powerless.

That is the reason I am writing this book and why I am so passionate about helping you change the lens through which you look at your life, so you can live with as much joy and wonder as your five-year-old self did. So, you can live a life of excitement and adventure. So, you can unleash your Inner Millionaire and impact millions! I know that if you can change your perception, you can change your life. And I know we change our perceptions through changing our belief systems. I am going to help you to do this because your significance is a birth right, your innocence is without question, and prosperity is equally available to everyone.

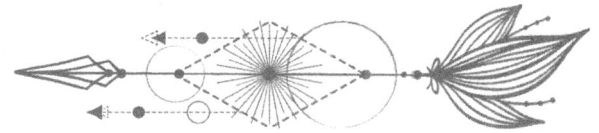

YOUR UNLEASHED VISION (& RECONNECTION TO YOUR SOUL GOAL)

"Hope rises like a Phoenix from the ashes of shattered dreams."
S.A. SACHS

A Soul Goal feels like a deep purpose that is etched into your DNA. It has always been with you. Perhaps for lifetimes. It is a deep desire that never really goes away and the indicator of whether you are living the life of your dreams or a life that feels misaligned and unsatisfying.

This book tells the story of where my Soul Goal began and shares how it got off course because of an identity of poverty that ran so deep to the core of me that the freedom to pursue the things that were important to me were ultimately always trumped in priority by the need to make money, create security and feel safe.

You might be in that exact position right now, reading this book, where you have a feeling deep in your soul that you are here to make a profound difference in the world. You know you are a **Thought Leader** with passions and impact goals, but they keep falling second place to the safety and security you feel you need to create.

You are working too hard; you are anxious and in constant hyper alert to "get things done." This is leaving you feeling unfulfilled and like there is more to life that you should be living.

My own experience of this stress and hustle led me ultimately back full circle to the impact I'd originally wanted to make as a coach. Now I am helping visionary Light Leaders to increase their income and impact and am a kaitiaki (Guardian) to the world's most challenged rainforests. My journey demonstrates that our journey to our truth may not be along a straight line, but in the twists and turns, there is always purpose and hope must not be extinguished because everything is possible.

A big part of my Soul Goal has also always been to write.

I have always seen writing as a platform to share powerful messages, but I used to get started on various projects and would finish none of them. As a child, my stories were always elaborate stories that had no conclusion. I was a Press Pack Reporter.

A Press Pack was a rite of passage for a British kid in the nineties. You could order your "Press Pack," a kit with a notepad and pen and you could write stories that could be featured on BBC television. I never actually got onto TV to be a Press Pack

Reporter, but in my imaginary games, my reporter pad and pen went everywhere. I was on a mission.

I discovered when I must have been just six or seven, from my best friend at school, that there were animals all over the world that were losing their lives and homes to deforestation. She came into school with a certificate showing this beautiful dolphin she had just adopted. It was like she opened up a whole new world to my eyes! My friend had the certificate because she was a supporter of the WWF, The World Wildlife Fund, and so, I wanted to be one also.

I begged my mum to sign me up, and one of the first animals I adopted was a formidable and incredible Silverback Gorilla. I would receive regular updates about how my donations were helping to protect them and always look forward to the monthly letter in the post. A few years later, my cousin travelled to see the Silverback Gorillas in the Congo. I was 13, and I remember the day I received his photos in the mail. The picture was taken so close up that I felt like my heart stopped; it was so incredible. I would make a trip like that one day.

Gorillas were my favourite animal, and it broke my heart to know that they were so threatened by forest clearance and degradation. I felt like it was my Soul Goal to help them and every other creature threatened by human impact. The dream of travel and conservation continued to call to me as I grew up, and I always felt called to write, like I had something important to say, but I always got stuck in the feeling that my creations needed to have some sort of structure. Like I needed to understand what the hell I was going to write about or have some sort of "plot." I would get wound up like a tight spring in this creative adventure, and the words would never flow.

That pretty much represents where my life ended up too, so bound tight by my own limiting beliefs and behaviours, and so in need of control, that nothing was flowing at all. I was anxious, drowning in the experience of financial lack and failing to hit any goals at all.

In 2018, I finally recognized the car crash of thoughts in my head, and the spin of emotions in my heart, and I began to question them. I questioned whether I could continue with all the inner turmoil I was experiencing. I recognized that what I was thinking was most likely the reason nothing was changing year after year in my life, despite everything I tried.

I guess, at some point, we all come to a position where we have the opportunity to question our beliefs. This position appears as discomfort. When life doesn't seem "enough" anymore. When things don't seem to "make sense" anymore. When we start to really feel our potential is untapped, and we wonder … why? We start to ask BIG questions like, "Who am I?" "Why am I really here?" "What is the value I was born to deliver and the impact I was meant to make?" And even … "Why am I doing these things that don't serve me in my life?"

Maybe this position appears when life starts to feel like a rollercoaster. The intensity of the ups and downs starts to make you feel ready to get off. Maybe you lose your grip, and the rollercoaster throws you off and you end up crashed and burned, and questioning what beliefs led you to wherever you are—stuck, broke, in an unhappy relationship or alone. Questioning … "What am I missing?" That's why you are reading this book, right? Something is missing. You are feeling a lack. The scarcity of something … but what? Is it money? Is it love? Or is it just the feeling of an inner void, like an inner knowing there should be more in your life.

Feeling a scarcity of something will cause you to hold onto what you do have like there is an award for it. Lack will become your identity. Even if you create money and experience abundance on the surface—good salary, nice house, nice car—if you are hustling to create this money and struggling to hold onto it, this is not abundance. Abundance is the ability to "have it all and have it easily." Abundance creates abundant choice because there is a greater force in the Universe working for you IF you can give up the fear that was created from the scarcity you experienced in the past, so you can truly live in the present moment where everything is possible and there is an abundance of everything.

Let me help you understand this better.

My mum and dad had quite the riches-to-rags tale.

My dad was an entrepreneur. He had a string of businesses that I remember went quite well when we were young. I remember his big warehouse that was like a house of treasures. At one point, it was filled from bottom to top with perfume that you could smell before you walked in. Another time it was filled with mobile phones, and I thought that was the coolest thing ever. My dad loved to be ahead of the curve and used to love to jump on the next "big thing."

I used to love sitting on my dad's big black leather chair. I would spin around and around on it. Mum would take us to the warehouse on the way home from school. We'd arrive in our shiny blue Scirocco with the top down and be excited for the opportunity to play. Dad worked a lot of hours. Mum worked with him too. I remember him coming home late, and we would run at his legs, as he came through the door, as we were on our way to bed in our pyjamas.

We had nice holidays and went to private, same-sex schools. We (my younger brother and I) had a holiday home that we absolutely adored in a forest-covered adventure playground in Worcestershire. We took it all for granted. That was just how life was and the children we played with who invited us over for playdates, also had those things, only bigger and better.

Now I know my dad was working to hold onto a life he probably couldn't afford and that it was really hard work to keep that lifestyle alive. There was no freedom in the life we were living. My dad's vehicle to make money was a rope around his neck. At some point, something happened, and everything changed.

I remember it was a rainy day at the end of summer. My brother and I had been playing in the lounge and Mum, Dad and my nan walked in looking really sober-faced. I panicked because the last time I had seen my parents look this way, they had shared the news that my grandfather had passed away and my nan would be coming to live with us. It couldn't be news like that again, could it?

I remember feeling tears start to burn my eyes. Mum or Dad, or both, I can't really remember, explained to me that we were going to move into our holiday home for a little while, and we would be changing schools. None of it made any sense really, but before we'd even had time to digest it, the change was underway.

We went from our beautiful five-bedroom house in Birmingham to a little three-bed chalet—the holiday home in Worcestershire—and that September I walked up to the local middle school and had the shock of my life. There were boys there, and the girls looked terrifying. I didn't know anyone, and everyone talked differently than me. I felt completely lost.

Did you ever have a nightmare where you walk into a room full of people and then you realise you are naked? It is the most uncomfortable dream as you feel their eyes burning holes through your skin. Everybody is staring. You feel completely vulnerable and exposed. That is how I felt that Monday morning as all those big eyes stared at me walking into my new classroom, but to be honest, it was the same feeling I'd had in the private school too. This feeling like I just didn't "fit in." Before I knew it though, a kind girl called Julia said there was space for me to sit down by her if I liked, and immediately, she introduced me to a beaming ginger-haired girl called Lydia and both are friends I hold dear to my heart to this day.

I don't really keep in touch with anyone from the previous nine years of my school life, only one girl who I think fit as badly into the private school setting as I did, and her name was Iona. She and I stuck out like sore thumbs, and we were forever in trouble. Life was one big adventure, and we were determined to take the journey.

A violin lesson outside of class became a challenge to skip it and see how long it took our teachers to notice. I remember we were discovered in the toilets bouncing rubber balls up the old brick walls, and we got into so much trouble! The school gardens with their boundaries were an invitation to see where we could escape. Our imaginations had no limits, and our play was free and filled with fun.

Iona's home life was very different from mine. Her mum was very strict and very proper. I don't think she thought much of me and my family. It was like however hard my dad worked to create a "shiny" life for us ... our poverty identity—the scarcity Dad was so afraid of—was a dirt we all couldn't wash off.

I'll never forget the time my mum came to pick me up from Iona's house, and she assumed she was being invited in and then Iona's mum blocked the doorway. It's crazy to think that before I was even 10 years old, I might have been experiencing classism that was shaping my view of people and their "place."

I know that Iona's dad worked hard like mine. He was a high-paid lawyer or accountant or something in a big firm. He was a lot softer than Iona's mum, and I remember he would come into our house and spend quite a lot of time chatting to my mum when he picked Iona up. Mum later told me she thought this might have been some sort of escapism from his high-pressure life at work and at home.

When Iona and I were in our late 20s, her dad committed suicide. There were no warning signs of it. They just woke up one day, and he was gone. Iona's life was turned upside down as she became the fulcrum of their family. Her mum had never done the family accounts or looked after the household matters and was drowning in her own grief and guilt. It's incredible that life can change like this in an instant. As fast as the snap of a branch, your world can completely fall around you, and you can freeze in the fall.

This was our experience in Worcestershire. Dad stayed in Birmingham to try and hold onto our house while my mum, my nan, my brother and I got to grips with life in this tiny chalet. Mum started working evenings in a restaurant. James and I just tried to get used to our new schools and make friends.

It was hard to watch my mum struggle without the money she'd been used to, grieving for the life that she had lost. She felt ashamed of the way our life had been downgraded and I believe this was the reason Dad fought so hard to hold onto what was left. Mum told me he was sleeping on the floor in our old house as one by one the furniture disappeared around him.

All the scarcity Dad had feared ... we were living it. Money was really scarce.

I can still feel the embarrassment of being laughed at on a non-uniform day early on in my new school life. As a pre-teen, I didn't know anything about the labels on clothing, but I'd seen the girls wearing certain things and wanted desperately to fit in. Mum couldn't afford the labelled clothes, so she bought me replica clothes instead.

I remember walking into the classroom feeling awesome because I thought I looked like everyone else did, but the girls all burst out laughing because I stuck out like a sore thumb instead with some random replica label on my flared jeans and a t-shirt that was obviously fake. I wanted to go home but had to endure the whole day in my unfashionable clothes instead.

That experience, and others from that time, where money became extremely tight, created the belief deep within me that money was really important to safety and security. It always felt like there wasn't enough. Paying the bills was a subject that created high stress. Money was scarce to buy new things like clothes. The regular holidays we used to take became a thing of our past and struggle became our new normal. It makes sense that right there grew the strong roots of my Scarcity Mindset, and I'm going to share through this book how this mindset seriously affected the decisions I made long into the future.

I would say no to things that might cause me to "lack more" and say yes to the things that promised me safety and security, even if they didn't feel aligned. I would make decisions and take actions from a place of lack, rather than from a place of abundance. Again, abundance is the belief that there is always enough.

I've realised that most of the decisions I have made in my life up until now have been made from a mindset that there is not enough. I now understand that lack became my identity even though there was so much focus on money and wealth when I was a child. Money held status, and lacking money was frowned upon and dangerous.

My memories of Mum and Dad when they had money are happy memories. Nice clothes, nights out, nice things, nice house. My memories after they lost everything are a lot darker—stress, lacking and worry. I didn't see the struggle Dad had to make money and hold onto money. I just saw the fruits of his labour and saw him chasing opportunities to make more money. Money was a good thing to have, and I experienced the pain of a world without money to get by.

Through this lens, my Money Blueprint was created—the belief that money was generally a scarce thing that you must work hard to get enough of and life without it is painful. This is the Blueprint that dictated my actions and decisions as I grew up, and this took me out of alignment with the truth of who I truly am—A Free Wild Adventurous Spirit with a Soul Goal to save the planet and the little girl who would skip out of violin class because she loved the danger of the unknown.

When I fell from that tree when I was 8 years old, the week following was awful. I was so physically uncomfortable. It hurt to pee, it hurt to walk, and sitting down was horrible. That experience made me cautious. It demonstrated to my innocent, 8-year-old self that life had risks. It made me believe that I had to be a little bit more cautious about my safety and life's potential dangers.

Many years down the line, I had a devastating experience that completely changed how I viewed the world and my security within it. It made me believe that nowhere was safe, and nobody could be trusted. It made my feelings about diving forth into the adventure of life very wary and fearful. I will share what this experience was later in the book.

For now, I need you to trust that whatever struggle you are facing right now, it is a gift that you must pay attention to because you have attracted it into your life. There are no such things as coincidences. You are right where you are meant to be based on the energy you are putting out.

That energy comes from your thoughts that come from your very own **Blueprint**.

If you are struggling in love, you have a Blueprint that was created from every experience you have had with love. If you are struggling with financial lack, you have a Blueprint that was created through every experience you have had with money and whatever Blueprint you have started with the experiences you had with your parents. The foundation of your Blueprint is their Blueprint.

Like the operating system of a computer, your Blueprint is the programming that creates your mindset and thinking.

And your thoughts are not just words spinning around your head, they carry powerful energy that drives the intention of everything you do and don't do and this is also a magnet to the experiences you have. Every thought you have (and therefore, every intention) has two components: it's **content** (those words spinning round your head) and ENERGY because everything is energy.

By directing your thoughts and focus to the struggle in your life, you are first blocking off the positive exchange of energy in your life and second, attracting the experiences you have. If you are negative, your experiences will be negative. If you are desiring the opposite, if you are craving abundance and for your "luck to change," your energy has to be in tune with your intention, otherwise your intention will never eventuate.

And INTENTION is non-negotiable. You have to want to turn things around. This desire also carries such a powerful energy that things can change in your life just by feeling it! My story will prove this. You will hopefully see, once you have read it, how what you are experiencing right now are unconscious self-defeating patterns that come from your limiting Blueprint.

The good news is that if the power in the energy of your thoughts and feelings can create the struggle in your life that you have, it means you can use the same power of your thoughts to gain the empowering perspective that will change everything in your life for the better and into alignment with your Soul Goal.

When I realised this, I felt angry with my mum and dad. I had this frustrating feeling that if only they could have looked at things differently when we were kids, everything would have been different, and we wouldn't have lived through the struggle that we did.

However, I needed to live through that struggle. I am here and able to share my learnings with you because of it. You can see my journey from an identity of poverty and lack to becoming the *Millionaire Sha'Woman* and trust that the capacity is within you too especially if you are experiencing financial lack like I was, feel alone or feel like you are failing in your goals. By the **Law of Energy**, and specifically, the **Universal Energetic Law of Polarity**, you can have and do the opposite just by changing how you look at things because how you look at things changes how you feel, which changes how you think, which changes what you attract, which how you take action!

Let me share a quick example of how powerful this **Law of Energy** can be and how quickly it can create change for you.

Aubrey came to me as a client in my *Awakened Wealth Breakthrough Programme*. I began talking about the idea of "Awakened Wealth" in 2022 after I experienced something that changed my intention around money forever (again, you will read about this experience later in the book). I realised how being wealthy is not about money at all, it is about having abundant choice, i.e., not living the experience my dad did, always hustling to make money and struggling to hold onto it, but about believing that there will always be enough if you are in energy as if there already is.

Many of the most famous "Manifestors" and **Law of Attraction** leaders talk about this—about living in the energy of what you want as if you have it already but I realised that very few show you HOW to do this in a practical way. My *Awakened Wealth Breakthrough Programme* shows you how and as part of it, you get a powerful 1:1 consultation with me where we do the very important process required to successfully manifest what you want, which is setting an UNLEASHED VISION of what it looks like.

"UNLEASHED" literally means releasing yourself from the limits of your Blueprint and setting a vision as if everything is possible in your life. When I undertook this process with Aubrey, she was shocked! She went from wanting to earn a little bit more money as a massage therapist to seeing herself owning her own therapy centre, with employed massage therapists and a gym, with corrective exercise and personal trainers.

When I asked her how much money she would be making in this vision, she started to add up how much she would need to pay for the space and pay the therapists. I asked her to let her logical mind go for a moment and feel how much money she would want to live an aligned life of abundance outside of the centre and pay for the centre as well, of course. Aubrey had stated in her visualisation that she would only be at the centre sporadically, checking in that everything was working okay. Aubrey said, $250K/month.

I asked her what this would feel like, and she said she would feel on top of the world, as if things were easy and in flow. And that is the crux of manifestation. When you can feel like something is possible and feel it like it has already happened, it will.

EVERYTHING IS CREATED TWICE BUT FIRST IN OUR IMAGINATION

So, take a moment to think about what would be possible for you if you were to be able to unleash yourself from your limiting Blueprint, set an unleashed vision and feel it in your body as if it was already happening in your life.

PRACTICAL INTEGRATION

JOURNALING EXERCISE

Look at your life as if you are looking at it through a lens and take a mental snapshot.

Can you identify the negative beliefs locked into your subconscious Blueprint that are blocking you from living out your unleashed vision? These beliefs might be that you're not good enough to succeed or not attractive enough to find love or you might see certain blocks outside of you. How are these beliefs, created by your past experiences, shaping the energy of your intentions? How have you attracted the life that you have through the energy of your thoughts? And how you are sabotaging your own potential and limiting the impact you can have on the world by how you feel and what you believe?

SET YOUR UNLEASHED VISION - Who is the Millionaire in you unleashed from all the limiting stories and beliefs above? What is the life you would be living? What is the money you would be earning? What is the impact you would be having? And how would you bring your life back into alignment with your Soul Goal?

Money is called currency because it is meant to flow. It comes in, it goes out. Is money something that you have negative emotions around? Can you connect those emotions to experiences you have had in the past? If you answer yes to both those questions, then congratulations because you are just about to change your life.

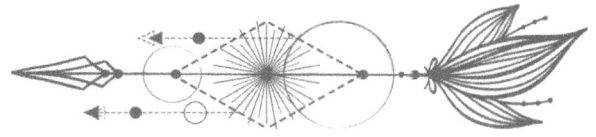

WORK WITH YOUR BRAIN
(INSTEAD OF AGAINST IT)

"We have to keep breaking our heart
until it opens."
RUMI

I am fascinated by the brain. My mum was diagnosed with bipolar disorder and suffered with debilitating bouts of mental illness that affected me a lot through my childhood. Mum's condition definitely changed how I saw the world. I developed a cynical view of people and experiences, and I judged my own emotions. There was a lot of stigmas attached to "being high" and "being low," so I tried to stay strong. I believed that I needed to.

Mum's reactions to life taught me that we are powerless to our world and our circumstances. As I grew up, I then also suffered with my own mental and emotional health because of what I'd learned subconsciously from my experiences growing up. My mind and my emotions became my enemy.

There's a Rumi quote that says, "We have to keep breaking our heart until it opens," which to me means that you will keep experiencing the same painful patterns that we talked about in the opening chapters of this book until you allow yourself to experience the vulnerability of what you fear.

THIS IS 100% A "BRAIN THING!"

Safety is a primal instinct and this primal instinct isn't logical.

For example, I have many clients come to me who say they fear failure ... but when we dig into their subconscious and start to reveal their limiting beliefs about themselves and the world they live in, they see how they actually fear success.

Success is unfamiliar whereas all of us tend to know failure quite well! This simply means that failure is familiar and a safe place to be and so we will unconsciously sabotage becoming successful.

This may look like struggling to stay consistent in a task that you know will shift the needle in your income or even manifesting physical illness before a job interview so that you can't go. Lack of clarity is the perfect self-sabotage; it's your gift from a brain that is desperately trying to keep you safe.

Your brain is extremely clever. It will keep you safe, even if it means making you miserable. I fondly call this being "comfortably miserable." Ultimately, "safe" often means the "same."

The hurts of past relationships will make us wary of who we allow into our lives, so we will choose to be alone, even if it makes us miserable. If we fear being alone, we will settle for relationships that are toxic and/or love for the wrong reasons. The pain of a broken heart will stop us opening ourselves up fully to the love of another, so again we will repeatedly choose loneliness or failing relationships. The shame of a previous embarrassment will haunt us for years to come and hold us back from putting ourselves out there in situations that could lead to the original embarrassment or feelings of shame. Even holding onto the belief that we are innately bad or broken or believing that abuse is our fault is a mechanism of safety because it creates a false sense of autonomy. The situation becomes "about you," which means you can control it, which makes it safe.

Let me take you back to me and the tree I fell out of as a child.

One single event changed my perception of it, taking it from exciting and enticing to threatening. The size of the tree never changed and I never once thought to question my ability to climb it in my decision never to be so stupid to climb trees again. My perception of the reality of the tree and its risks changed the minute I fell out of it. I no longer believed in the innocence of the adventure. Instead, I believed in the warnings of my mum that climbing trees is dangerous. As I hit the bike frame and felt that pain reverberate between my legs and through my body, this became the truth in my reality. Climbing trees is dangerous. And this is how our beliefs are formed—from a dramatic emotional impact that imprints a new truth in the moment in the brainstem.

The "Reticular Activating System" (RAS) is a bundle of nerves at your brainstem that then seeks out information from your environment and experiences you are in that validate your beliefs, and it filters out all the unnecessary information to make sure that the information vital to your survival gets through. It basically filters your world through the parameters of your belief systems, so that what you focus on, you see.

In 2017, I had gotten to the same place financially that my parents had arrived to—struggling to find money to eat. I had been frantically trying to grow a home business after I had lost my job when I was six months pregnant with my second child. I was too pregnant to be a favourable candidate for a similar job to the one I had lost, working for a trust within a school, and so I was forced to work for minimum wage in a retail store.

We began to struggle financially because when we had bought our house, we'd had two full-time wages, and now there was only one wage coming in. My husband was trying hard to make ends meet, and I was trying hard to find the magic bullet that would make my home business a success, but we had been living outside of our means for a while and soon, even the credit card wasn't stretching enough to cover our outgoing expenses.

When I lost my job, my initial reaction had been to feel angry and bitter at my employers because they had taken my entitlement to maternity leave away. However, now I see how I was actually in a place of deep need, just like my parents had been, and I was directly following their pattern of being a victim to my circumstance, believing I was powerless to do anything to change it and martyring myself to that belief. If I'm honest, now I can see how the way I was working in my business was from a place of avoiding scarcity instead of servicing the burning desire I felt to make a difference in the world. And the irony was that I wasn't making a difference to myself or my children who needed me either, and everything was lacking anyway.

One day, I went to the supermarket to try and get milk, bread, and some veggies to tide us through to my husband's payday, and my credit card was declined at the checkout. The feeling of embarrassment was like my heart stopping. Electric shocks radiated through my body. This was the moment I had feared. I think I already knew that we had maxed out the card limit, but I didn't know what else to do but to try and get some food to put in my girls' bellies. They were hungry.

I opened the fridge, and it was empty. I opened the pantry, and it was empty. I opened the freezer, and even that non-descript box of something I had frozen many moons ago and had not labelled was gone. We were out of everything, and we would have eaten anything. I remember in my panic thinking that maybe there would be some miracle saving grace in a generous stranger in the supermarket. Or maybe I'd win some "on the spot" competition for being the 100th customer on the store's birthday. Or maybe the shopping would just miraculously go through the checkout anyway. That stuff happens, right?

I was so embarrassed when the card was declined that I just ditched my shopping, grabbed the girls' hands, and fled the supermarket. I felt like if I stopped, I'd either throw up, pass out or both. I felt like the supermarket was trying to swallow me. The exit seemed so far away. Both my children were screaming.

The supermarket was already my enemy. It was like some drug I couldn't stop taking. I knew I had to go there and give into filling my trolley with food, but the exercise of paying for it had been getting more and more painful, the closer we had come to being broke. During a few of my previous shopping trips, I had just lost it completely with my children just for being children and doing what children do. I hated myself for snapping at them like that, but the experience of shopping had become harrowing. I was becoming a mirror of my own mum, a victim to my stress and inability to manage my emotions.

Because of this experience, most things had become harrowing for me. It was like I was waiting to be given a death sentence that was inevitable. I felt anxious constantly. I was always waiting for that final card to stop handing out money that wasn't ours.

I couldn't tell anyone because I felt so much shame. Craig's parents were away travelling at the time things got really bad, so I couldn't reach out to them. I'm not sure I would have anyway because of my pride. That day, after the card declined, I went home and cried. My children were still asking for something to eat.

In a moment of pure despair, I knew I had to reach out for help. Thankfully, our little town had a food bank, and I swallowed my pride enough to go and ask for help. It was the best thing I could have done. As I cried and hugged the lifeline who welcomed us in with open arms, my children ripped into a box of cereal and started eating it with their bare hands. I was mortified. I had been so blinded by my own stress and shame that I hadn't seen what they needed. I hadn't noticed the extent of their hunger. How long had I been avoiding afternoon tea and snacks to avoid seeing the truth of our situation? This was the lowest point I think I have ever experienced in my life, even after everything else. The pain of letting my children down was something that stayed with me for a really long time.

Is there some irony in that I ended up in this position? Just like my parents?

The answer is no. I feared scarcity, and scarcity was where I wound up, knee-deep in it because it was my focus.

At the time, just like my parents, I didn't know that there was an alternative to being a victim to my situation and because of this, on that day in May 2017, I had a tough road ahead of me as I stepped out of that food bank with my boxes full of food and a heart full of hope. Thankfully though, my energy was silently asking for a MIRACLE.

When I had dropped to my knees sobbing as my kids tore into the box of cereal with their bare hands, I had set a powerful intention from the core of myself that had said, "I don't know how, but everything is going to change."

I've always had this innate tenacity ...

That weekend, I went to my normal market stall where I sold soaps and other things I made from natural ingredients and essential oils. This was my first (and failing) venture into entrepreneurship after I had been made redundant from the school trust and I got to the end of another day where my sales weren't going to leave a profit after I paid for the stall.

I was sitting staring hopelessly into space when a lady came up to me and said, "You look like somebody who is into health and wellness, you should take a look at this!" She handed me a card with a website on it. Ordinarily I would have smiled politely and chucked the card in the bin, but today I was drawn to look at the website, so I opened it up on my phone. It shared a page full of videos about this new wearable technology that claimed to help you hit your health and wellness goals using personalised artificial intelligence.

I was fascinated. The videos talked about how your body had a voice and you could listen to it, so you could make proactive choices that would make you feel better and live better. The idea of being able to listen to the messages in the anxiety that was crippling me every day was appealing. Nothing I had tried by that point had taken the anxiety away. My essential oils had helped take the edge off, but the medication I had used previously, the counselling, therapy and other things I'd tried had never brought true healing, and I was tired.

The website also shared how there was a business opportunity attached to the technology. You could get paid to wear and share the technology! I watched every single video on the website before I had left the market and when I got home, I showed them all to my husband. Within a few days, we had accessed a fresh credit card and bought into the technology opportunity and by the end of the week, I was under the safe wings of my miracle. Her name was Lesley.

Lesley was my upline in the company and an amazing coach, speaker and author. Everything about her made my eyes open wider, and she immediately began to get me questioning my beliefs and exploring the new habits I could integrate to make changes in my life.

I remember she asked me, "Well, Clare, if you don't want the reality that you have, what is the reality you want?" and I couldn't answer her question. All I could see was black. This is another safety mechanism of the brain because of its resistance to the unsafety of uncertainty and the unknown. But meeting Lesley was my first gift from the Universe because her gentle coaching helped me to push through the inertia that I felt, and I slowly began to see a picture of a life that felt good.

Wearing the technology, I also started to see the things in my environment that were making me feel bad—the whispers from my body that I hadn't been able to listen to, meaning that my body was screaming out through the anxiety— "I feel unsafe!!"

This wasn't my first experience with coaching because I had trained to be a Life Coach the previous year, but never managed to integrate the skills into my business model profitably. I was charging 30 pounds an hour for coaching sessions and not even succeeding to sell them.

Lesley was an incredibly adept coach and showed me the true power of coaching to change a person's life, which changed the value I saw in it. She introduced me to the potential of the brain and demonstrated the true power of being a woman. She was the antidote to the powerlessness of my mum and her wisdom, spirituality, and grace rocked my world.

Coaching is like walking into and out of a bucket, and the content of the bucket is the landscape of your internal world. If you imagine a bucket in front of you, the lip of the bucket closest to you is where you are now, and as you start to walk down the inside of the bucket you discover the internal landscape that is creating the blocks you have, and this enlightenment ignites the glimmers of opportunity to improve your life.

Coaching takes you away from need and towards desire and choice. So many of us are stuck in a survival mode making decisions simply out of need, just like I was, but from the place of an intention for something to be different in your life, a good Coach can take you deep into the contents of your bucket until you find enlightenment. Each step deeper into your bucket's contents is prompted by a question from your

Coach who will keep going until there are no more questions to ask because you have found the answers you need to make positive changes. Then you will start walking up to the other side of your bucket into the light with solutions and with hope. You will have cut loose from the things that were holding you back, and before you know it, you will be standing in a completely different place, broken free from the past, ready to go forward with life.

Coaching is like holding a mirror up to your life. Seeing your life through your Coach's lens helps you see the things you weren't able to before, and the Coach's empowering questions will help you see things from a different perspective, so that you can take different actions with new enthusiasm and create different outcomes in your life.

You can take this journey too, but it starts with the same full body intention that I felt in the food bank. I don't believe you have to hit rock bottom before you do this, but as Rumi implies … Maybe continuing to break your heart until it opens is the rite of passage to life finally changing. In my moment of intention, I made a commitment to myself and my children. Our life was going to change. I couldn't live another day with the crippling anxiety that was killing me. And I was ready to receive the powerful education Lesley gave me about my brain.

She shared how between the age of 0 and 7 years old, our brain is in a "theta" brainwave state, like a sponge that simply absorbs information and does not question it. Across these first seven years is where we create our most debilitating limiting belief systems about ourselves and about the world simply because we don't have the reasoning ability to discern the truth in the situations we are experiencing. This "theta" brainwave state is used by hypnotherapists because it is such an impressionable state of mind, and it means their subject will do and think whatever they suggest to them.

I'm sure you have giggled like I have at stage acts where a bunch of grown adults walk around clucking like chickens. Between 0 and 7, we are literally in this state constantly, and we have no ability in our brain to question anything. We watch our parents and how they experience events, and we absorb the "intel" from all of it.

Our experiences, how we experience them and the conclusions we make create the internal operating system—the Blueprint—that directs us in our experiences as adults. By adulthood, our thinking mind is producing over 70,000 thoughts a day, and 85% of them are the same thoughts we had yesterday believe it or not! Our behaviour is driven by our thoughts. Which means 85% of what we do every day is pre-programmed by our habitual thinking, which is driven by the beliefs programmed into our internal operating system, our Blueprint.

"Neuroplasticity" is the quite recent scientific discovery that our brain can adapt and change as a result of new experiences and new ideas. Thanks to Neuroplasticity, while we can have this "bad wiring," the very process through which we created it in the first place means we can etch in new positive programming by intentionally creating new experiences and new habits.

That is why personal development is so powerful. It is the process of changing our beliefs, born out of our past experiences, by integrating new positive habits on a daily basis. However, it is not easy because of the same inertia I experienced before Lesley miraculously appeared in my life, and most people will fail to change their life for this very reason. And yet, the very same brain that is creating your inertia can be the gift that unleashes your Inner Millionaire.

WHEN YOU LEARN HOW TO WORK WITH IT, INSTEAD OF AGAINST IT.

This is the first key difference between me and my mum. I learned how, and she did not.

For a huge part of my life, I believed that her bipolar disorder was something we couldn't change. And believe me, I tried! In fact, I think the fact that I could never fix her was the reason I walked out of childhood with such a deep Soul Goal to go fix the world instead.

Now I know that my mum was just let down within a system that is scared to look at the real possibilities of the brain. As you will read in the later chapters of this book, the possibilities of your brain can make you superhuman. And a bunch of superhumans walking around our planet would be very bad for a governmental system that controls us based on the brain's primary instinct to keep us safe from scarcity and the other things we fear.

When my mum and dad were struggling financially, they looked to this system to support them and it didn't, and so their journey ended there. They didn't know to look to the power deep within themselves because access to the information that would have taught them to do that was not widespread at the time. In the present day, it still isn't, but science is changing, mainstream thinking about the possibilities of the brain is changing, and people are learning that we can "unplug from the Matrix" and take back our full, divine and sovereign power as human beings.

The irony is that our full, divine and sovereign power as human beings is ancient wisdom that can be seen as far back as cave paintings. The breathwork modality I chose to use as part of the transformational coaching journey I began in 2021 is based on a story from the ancient times of Rigveda back in 1500 B.C. It is said that the Rigveda people realised the power of their own minds when they were forced to stop taking a plant medicine that was helping them receive the "divine downloads" that would take humanity forward. They ate so much of a plant they called "Soma" that it ran completely out. Then, someone realised they could access the same divine intelligence with the power of their breath. And as I teach you in the third part of this book, this is exactly how I accessed my *Miracle Frequency* and started manifesting abundance WITH EASE, and I show you how you can **Crack Your Own Abundance Code** in the same way and start changing your own life and destiny in under an hour a day.

But you are going to have to overcome your own inertia first, and it starts with changing your belief systems.

PRACTICAL INTEGRATION

JOURNALING EXERCISE

SET INTENTION

Sit down somewhere that you will be undisturbed. Sit cross-legged on the floor if possible and face East.

Placing your hands in a prayer position and touching your thumbs to the third eye point on your head, take a deep breath in and then chant an "Ah - Ooh - Oom" sound on your out breath. As you chant each sound, feel its vibration, the "Ah" sound in your belly, the "Ooh" sound in your heart space and the "Oom" sound in your head behind your eyes. If you can, make the "oom" sound make a vibration in the area of your pineal gland in your brain.

If you can, lie forward, like a seated bow and place your forehead on the ground. Feel the energy of the earth beneath you and take another deep breath in, this time on your out breath, release any tension and allow your body to lie heavy on the ground.

Feel the intention within you to release from the victim consciousness that is keeping you stuck and causing you to see down a very narrow reality tunnel and preventing you from living a limitless version of your life.

Recall your UNLEASHED Vision and as you sit back up straight, breathe in deeply again and this time, squeeze your pelvic floor and feel energy move up your spine, bring the picture of your UNLEASHED Vision into your mind's eye.

Smile as you connect to how it would feel for this vision to realise itself and as you breathe in one final time, again squeeze energy up from your pelvic floor and feel it move up your spine. Hold the energy as you hold your breath at the top and feel the power of your intention to break your limiting patterns and unleash your Inner Millionaire.

Your integration is complete.

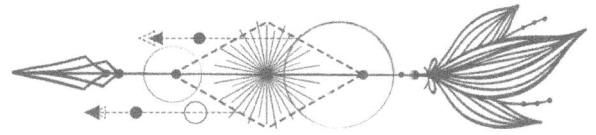

DECIPHER YOUR ABUNDANCE CODE

"How can you show up so you're picked first."
RAY HIGDON

Now you are starting to see why even those with the deepest Soul Goal to create positive change in the world play small and stay stuck in income plateaus. They have limiting stories and beliefs that they don't know how to shift. And if you are a Coach, Thought Leader or any other person of authority, you may also have an ego that is telling you that you should have already sorted "your shit" out and be further ahead than where you are. And the scarcity that creates will be making you feel less inclined to turn your attention away from striving for more accomplishments and helping more people toward shifting your limiting beliefs. Am I right?

If I'm speaking to you, I want you to know that it's okay to be broken. We all are. We all have limiting beliefs, whatever level we are at, and true self-mastery requires bringing awareness to these beliefs and changing them. And every time you do, you will become more valuable to your clients as well.

If you truly want to decipher your **Abundance Code** like I did, it starts with breaking through your limiting beliefs, changing your reality tunnels and letting go of fear like I did.

There is a science behind the Law of Attraction, and it states that everything is a mirror of the frequency created by the emotions you are having every single day. Feel into the emotions you have experienced in the last 24 hours. Maybe you have been unable to switch off thinking about your business, and it has created feelings of anxiety. Maybe you have bills to pay and are worried over whether you will have the money to pay them, so you are feeling fear. Maybe the "shit has hit the fan" in some way, either personally or professionally, and you are feeling angry, bitter or scared. Maybe you are blaming people or blaming something outside of yourself for what is going on and are feeling resentful. Maybe you are pushing up against a deadline and feeling a scarcity of time, making you feel desperate. Maybe the deadline is causing you to not prioritise sleep and your self-care, and so you are feeling fatigued, unhealthy and lacking in a sense of inner peace.

All these feelings—resentment, anxiety, desperation, extreme fatigue, etc.—are low-frequency emotions. A great visual a Coach once gave me was to think of them all pouring out of your head like an antenna and everything in your physical world is just a reflection of their frequency.

In the **Law of Attraction**, like attracts like. So, if you are worrying about something, you are effectively praying for it to happen … If you are struggling, you will attract more struggle …

If you feel scarcity around money, then you will attract more scarcity of money ... And if you want the reflection to change, you must change your internal operating system—the Blueprint—created by your core belief systems because there is a ripple effect of consequences that are playing out from them and creating the reality you have.

With the belief my mum had that her Bipolar diagnosis was a life sentence, she also surrendered to her feelings and created the reality she experienced. An example is how she struggled to cope with being a mum to me and my brother. Unintentionally, because she had no remedy to the power of the emotions she felt (and there is no doubt in my mind now that those emotions were calling in more struggle), she lost her temper with us often and lashed out daily.

I have this vivid memory of my brother and I being asked to hang out in the lounge while she got her hair cut and for some unknown reason, I was intimidating my brother with a hairbrush, waving it at his head, threatening to hit him with it. Before I knew it, I actually had hit him and blood was spurting out everywhere! In a panic, I ran to my mum who was mid haircut and she went running into my brother, James. Of course, he looked a sorry sight.

She saw red and chased me up the stairs in a blind rage. I remember hiding behind the door of my bedroom and pushing it shut with all of my weight while she yelled and tried to get in through the door. I was terrified. I was surprised. I was confused. I knew what I had done was wrong. I just didn't get why she hated me so much for it.

I remember me and my brother often acting out like that and for a long time, I felt like I must have been a really bad kid. Now

I realise we were just being kids, and probably in some ways, we were seeking attention. It certainly didn't invite the right sort of attention, just lots of angry outbursts and volatility like that moment where Mum chased me up the stairs. I remember the fear in my body of what was coming.

I have another memory of my brother being curled up in the fetal position after being beaten by Mum for doing something he shouldn't have even though now I can't remember now what it was. I remember feeling so helpless and terrified at the same time. I wanted to step in and make her stop, but I didn't want to feel the pain of her hand turning to me.

Your body does not forget these memories of pain. They are imprinted into your brainstem and these imprints send messages to your nervous system so that it knows how to keep you alive.

If you imagine your nervous system as a ladder, there are three levels to it. The **"ventral vagal"** part of the nervous system is at the top of the ladder, which is where you sit when everything feels safe and social; the **"sympathetic"** part is in the middle of the ladder, which is where you "fall down" to when something seems threatening to your safety (you'll recognise the term for this, "fight or flight"); and the **"dorsal vagal"** part is at the bottom of the ladder, which is where the nervous system shuts completely down. This is the place we go to when there is no further down the ladder to go. Fighting or fleeing is futile, so we immobilise as the only way to protect ourselves. We see this in beetles when they flip onto their back and "play dead." When you have trauma, your nervous system can get stuck in a hypervigilant fight or flight state, or stuck in a frozen, immobilised state, or jump frantically between states. There is also a frequency to these states as they create certain emotions like anxiety and fear.

What I know as an adult is that my mum suffered extreme trauma in her childhood that she's never healed from. Because of this trauma, as a parent, her world became too overwhelming for her. She was definitely stuck in fight or flight, which causes the older "reptilian" part of your brain to kick into a survival mode, and this makes us very reactive. We go to emotions like anger by default as a protection mechanism instead of using the newer part of the brain, the neocortex, to come up with a more considered response that would create higher frequency emotions as well.

An example of this is when I get potential clients in front of me in sales calls who want a coach, but have also not done the internal work to heal their money fears They hear the investment for my coaching, and their mind goes directly into a survival response; they have never had that amount of money available before and so they say without thinking ... "I can't afford it." Those clients who have worked with me for a while and healed their limiting money beliefs and stories are not triggered by experiences in their past anymore, and so their brain does not need to kick into survival mode. Instead, there is space for a measured response. For example, a question they ask themselves is, "How can I afford this?"

This also allows the sympathetic nervous system to work in a healthy way to make you feel energised and mobilised for the challenge, but when this state is protective and unhealthy, you feel anxious, agitated, irritable and angry. You will react in unhealthy ways like having a panic attack, and when you have exhausted all defensive avenues, you will then disconnect and disassociate. Sometimes you can drop directly down from ventral vagus to dorsal vagus if the threat feels big enough, and I think this was what was happening with my mum. She disconnected and disassociated from us for her own protection because she couldn't cope. Then, when we threatened her, she was literally fighting to protect herself. Obviously, as children, we didn't experience this from a logical position because a young brain literally doesn't have the mental capacity. So, I first got the feeling from her reactions to things that everything in life was really hard. And I also got the feeling that I was in some way fundamentally flawed, and I felt ashamed.

Unfortunately, this feeling of shame grew with me as I grew up.

When I was in my early teens, my dad lost his business, and in the period that followed where my mum and dad lived mostly apart, I grew up a lot. When my dad moved back in with us, he didn't really know me anymore. I was a stranger to him, I think. I was now this grown-up girl who wore makeup, miniskirts, and had a mobile phone and a social life. I know now that he was also depressed. I don't know for sure, obviously, but I think he felt like he had failed us by losing our house and taking us out of private schools. He became very aggressive. I almost hate writing this because I don't want you to think badly of him. My dad is an incredible dad, and one of the strongest men I know with a heart the size of a lion that was filled with so much love for my mum. In this way, his biggest desire in life has always been to protect her.

When my dad met my mum, he was married to someone else. His wife introduced him to Mum, and Dad said from the moment he met her, he felt this responsibility to sort her life out. He protected her over everything. When my brother and I were young, we were a threat to Mum just by being kids.

Especially when we were teenagers and in periods when Mum wasn't coping well. Dad just wanted to make things easy for her. And in losing his business, things were hard. He was stressed. Maybe James and I were a handful. As an adult who now has felt the fear of all he had to lose, I get it. I get the short temper and the rage. But back then, I think it was just another piece of evidence to my subconscious that I wasn't good enough and evidence that I was fundamentally flawed.

Some days it felt like everything I did was wrong. I was me, but "me" wasn't helpful to anyone. I couldn't figure out what he needed me to be. It was confusing. Whatever I did didn't make things easier for he and my mum.

Neither James or I felt important over their financial struggle, and I think we both took meaning from this in terms of our safety and self-worth. I developed a deep lack of self-worth and decided a lot about my own potential on a subconscious level. This showed up in my teenage years as a longing that made me crave for love from men to feel protected and safe. Later in my life, it showed up as a craving for material wealth to feel protected and safe. And then, finally, it showed up as feelings of deep depression, anxiety and post-traumatic stress because I couldn't find the safety I was looking for, so I escaped from the pain this created with alcohol and by being busy until the anxiety started to hold me back from doing more things and then finally, life felt a lot safer, but ultimately, I had begun to exist in a safe bubble only and had given up playing big.

Beginning to write this book was so helpful in starting to see things like that. It was like putting the pieces of a jigsaw puzzle together and seeing the big picture behind all the actions I had and hadn't taken throughout my life. Everything started to make sense. For a long time though, I then battled with the idea of publishing it because I didn't want to paint the picture of my parents as bad people because they aren't. It's simply that nobody had shared with them that there were alternative ways or how they could have been the creative power to deal with the circumstances that life served them. Or that those circumstances were manifesting from the energy of their beliefs.

As I have shared, their state of powerlessness was a pattern I repeated in my own life, and I guess ultimately, that is what helped me to get over myself and publish ... was the opportunity to get the powerful message out that you can change your perspective and awaken your **Miracle Frequency** and that "having it all" is easier than you think.

My husband once said to me that he sometimes has a memory resurface, seemingly out of nowhere, about a time where he felt embarrassed, where he even admits there was probably no need for his embarrassment, but he felt it anyway. He asked me what I thought this could be, and I said that while he might not realise it, some feeling in the present will have triggered a subconscious memory from the past to surface. It could be something insignificant like the fleeting feeling of not being comfortable in a social setting or unconsciously questioning his worthiness in his job. However, that momentary discomfort would be enough to trigger his brain to pour through his old memories and find the evidence it needs to protect him from experiencing the pain of his past again.

Our brains are really smart. The brain is like a giant super computer. It isn't doing its job if it isn't protecting us. So, if something bad happens to us in our lives and we don't take the time, at the time, to figure out the true lesson in the experience, the brain will store a false truth that will keep us safe and hold us back, again and again.

We don't remember everything consciously. Only the moments that had a high emotional charge, either positively or negatively in the moment. Like me, you may not have many memories of childhood, but you remember the really good times and the really bad times. The rest are stories you reminisce over at Christmas or as you look over old family photo albums.

I became fascinated by the brain when I realised that mine was the very thing holding me back from a life of happiness.

Do you ever listen to a song and no matter what you are doing, how you are feeling, you wind up in tears? Whether you realise it or not, your subconscious has seen, heard, and held onto every single thing you have felt in the past. It has been aware of everything you have experienced emotionally even if you haven't been consciously paying attention. It has been absorbing every detail around you, every sound, every sense, all of the time.

When the words and sounds of a song play out that trigger an emotion from the past that is unhealed, your subconscious will register it and seek back into your brain "cloud" of every single bit of data it has ever absorbed. Then, it will instantly raise the emotion attached to whatever circumstance tied you to the song in the first place, and you will feel an emotion from the past all over again.

BOTTOM LINE: If we don't allow ourselves to feel emotions, they get stuck.

The song *Fix You* by Coldplay was always one of the songs I couldn't listen to without bursting into tears. In a subconscious reprogramming session, I locked onto the belief I held that I had failed my mum in some way by being unable to "fix her" and I realised the "untruth" in it. From this enlightenment, so much more clarity came through. I realised how the drama of the extreme ups and downs in the world I was growing up in was self-created. I wondered if in some weird way, Mum needed drama to justify the feelings that were all stacked up and stuck inside of her because she felt like she couldn't find any logical reason to feel them.

And again, I realised how as I had grown up, I had demonstrated the same pattern. I had created my own drama because drama felt familiar. I'd choose to seek drama out and let it envelope me until I could see nothing else. And tucked up in that envelope was a comfortable place I also knew how to live in. I didn't really know how to live without struggle. When stuff happened around me, I made it my focus. Family drama, friendship drama, work drama, even global drama on the TV! It was just another pattern in my life that I unconsciously repeated. And the frequency of the emotions that were created were mirrored by the external "lack" in my life.

When I made the decision to heal that story about my mum and believe that it was not my role to fix her and see that I had not failed her in any way, I could finally listen to Coldplay's song without sobbing. The sadness had transmuted itself, and I no longer felt this call to go backwards. I finally felt empowered with choices about how I could go forward as well.

I felt liberated to connect with my purpose on a whole new level of leadership and impact. It wasn't just my mum I couldn't fix. It was the whole world. I suddenly realised that wasn't my role and instead my role was to embody my own transformation and radical expression of my gifts and understand how I raise my frequency to one of unconditional love in all areas of my life. And I realised that doing this would be the fastest way to change everything in the world for the better.

PRACTICAL INTEGRATION

JOURNALING EXERCISE

Think about a dream that you have had that has made you feel uncomfortable. For example, I once dreamt that I joined friends in some natural pools and realised I was naked. Then, I went to my boot camp naked. And then when I drove home from boot camp, I was suddenly driving a double-decker bus that had the driver's seat upstairs. I couldn't see below me, the brakes were not working properly, and I was in the middle of London in the pedestrian part!

I got stuck down this alleyway, and I couldn't go backwards. I was at a fork in the path, and I could only go left or right.

I asked the people around me, which way should I go?

They answered, where are you going?

My husband then woke me up and said the clocks had changed, and that I needed to go running.

I dreamt this dream at a time when I was searching outside of myself for the answers to a business challenge, and nobody was providing them to me. I was being forced to trust in my own judgement, which challenged one of the biggest limiting beliefs I have carried about myself throughout my life, born out of that "fundamentally flawed" feeling I'd had since child-hood that "I get things wrong and make bad decisions." The idea that I had to trust myself to make a call on some really important things was punishing me!

Joe Dispenza says, "Don't focus on the events in the dream, focus on the feelings the dream creates.'

Feel whether you have a dream you can use to identify a limiting pattern of beliefs you have about yourself or the world you live in. Maybe you have a recurring dream you can interrogate. If you can't think of a dream, simply feel your limiting patterns of behaviour. Maybe you people please or struggle to say no. Maybe you always pivot in your business when it starts to get successful. Maybe you always blow money if you have it. What could be a limiting belief you have that if you could change it, your life would look totally different?

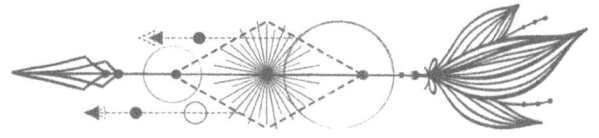

IDENTIFY YOUR ARMOURS

In 2003, I travelled to South America to spend a year teaching English in a school in Chile.

My interest in South America began when I was about 12 years old. I had seen a picture of Machu Picchu, and I remember asking, wide-eyed, whether such a wonderful place really existed and how I could get there.

From that day onwards, I was obsessed with Inca history and read many different books and even began to learn Spanish from an old phrase book that belonged to my mum. While discovering South America, I fell totally head over heels with the majesty of the Amazon rainforest and its power, beauty, and life. I was captivated by the seemingly infinite green forest, the diversity of species, and the magic of species yet to be known, and I was sooooo curious about indigenous lives.

Blessed with my trip to South America in 2003, I set the intention to understand what supporting the rainforest would look like. I would be spending my year abroad teaching, but I planned to visit the Amazon on my summer break to understand how I could support its conservation. The South America trip was part of my university course. I'd gone to university having no idea what I wanted to do on the other side of studying. I'd chosen Hispanic Studies as a course because teaching a language seemed like a secure career. The year abroad was to deepen my language skills and cultural experience. I could go to Spain or South America, and while I was there, I could teach or study. I literally chose teaching just so I would get paid, and South America so I could visit the Rainforest!

Mum and Dad looked at me bemused and anxious every time I spoke of my plans to travel to South America. I think part of them thought I would never actually go, and the other part of them hoped I wouldn't. Mum and Dad carried a generally dismal view of the world after they lost their home and business, and they consistently focused on all the bad things that happened in it, which made them terrified that something bad would happen to me.

I guess for them too, there was pressure because funding the trip was going to be challenging. I quite liked the hustle of supporting myself and saving for my year abroad. I actually felt like my dad, working hard for what I wanted. The year before I left for South America, I'd worked in a nightclub multiple nights a week and wouldn't finish until the early hours of the morning. Then, I would walk up into my lectures half asleep! (I'm pretty sure that's when I developed my love/addiction to coffee.) But deep down, it felt like this was just the way it was meant to be. Hard work pays off dividends, right?

The day it was finally time to get on the plane and actually go to South America, my heart burned with emotions—sadness at saying goodbye, but excitement about the adventure that lay ahead. While I hadn't had the easiest of relationships with my parents for one reason or another, they were my world, and I was still their little girl. I loved them (and still love them) with every part of me.

It was a really long drive from Birmingham down to Heathrow where I was picking up my flight, and my nerves started to rise as we hit the long tunnels that signalled arrival into Heathrow airport. The light at the end of the tunnel would be the departure part of the airport. Suddenly, the darkness of the tunnels wasn't the only darkness closing in on me. Suddenly, I was experiencing the thick, suffocating feeling of fear. Then, before I could blink, the dark tunnels were a haze behind me, and I realised there was no changing my mind on this decision I had made to be the nomad I'd always felt I truly was in my heart.

Even though both my Mum and Dad never finished school, they always made this massive deal about how important it is to go to school, get good grades and go to university because "this is how one gets the good jobs and is successful." I'm not saying they were the reason it took me until I was in my 20s to start living a little more in alignment with my big dreams, but they did begin to frame my belief that education is an important priority, and then those within my education framed my beliefs further about the careers that could give me a solid income and security. Security was a thing that was consistently made out to be of critical importance in life. Nobody really talked about happiness. Or freedom.

As we headed closer to the airport, Mum beamed at me from the front seat of the car. Could she sense it? Could she sense the fear I felt? She'd always joked she had a sixth sense. We'd laugh at how she would guess what I was thinking before I opened my mouth, and she was convinced that she could "feel it" before I rang her phone.

If I'm honest, I believe that Mum's bipolar disorder might have been an inability to cope with her spiritual gifts. If you look at the definition of "bipolar" it causes manic highs and lows. I don't really remember the manic times, only the deep, dark sadness and rage. (And how she never really saw the sunny side of life and her cup was always half empty.) From what I understand now about the possibilities of the brain, which I will share with you in the third part of this book, it would make a lot of sense that bipolar disorder would be diagnosed over the impact of spiritual gifts in someone who doesn't know how to properly deal with them!

In this moment, as she beamed at me from the front of the car, whether by sixth sense of my fear, maternal connection to my feeling of insecurity or by pure coincidence, her big white teeth gave me deep comfort.

Her smile had always been her most startling feature to me. When she smiled, it was this huge beaming smile, just like at that moment, and it seemed strange that she didn't smile all the time. I'd always thought my mum was so beautiful. For most of my life, she'd had this attractive pixie haircut that matched so well with her big green eyes and naturally olive skin that she worked so hard to darken in the summer. (She proudly told me stories of dousing herself in baby oil as a teenager to get a better suntan!)

Her smile was different though that day. I could see that behind it was the same uneasiness I was feeling. I wanted to grab hold of her like I used to when I was a small child. Whatever we had been through, she was the closest person to me in my whole life, and this would never change. I knew she could take the fear away, maybe stroke my hair gently and make everything okay, but I was stuck behind my seatbelt, and I didn't want her to see that I was afraid.

I was 21 years old at this point, and I felt like I was a fully-fledged adult that didn't have the right to grab hold of her, and I would have pulled away if she had embraced me. "Being strong" by this point was my default way to be. Moreover, I had imagined this moment for the better part of my life, and I wasn't going to crumble now. I repeated over and over, "I can do this," in my mind, but even I didn't believe myself as I said it. I could hear the words of my other friend from university echoing through me at the same time, "It'll all be fine!" That was his catch phrase, and it was always so comforting, but suddenly in that moment, it was not "cutting the biscuit."

Once we had arrived at the airport, dropped off my massively overpacked bag, and were heading to the departure gates, I realised it was finally time to say goodbye and my stomach churned. Was it hunger? Mum had always been neurotic about food, saying, "You won't get anything out if you don't put anything in," so we stopped off at the Wetherspoons outside the final departure gate, and she forced me to eat something. I'd normally love drinking the free pint of cold, refreshing lager, but at that moment, the soggy burger and curly fries just were not making saying goodbye to my parents any easier.

As Mum wrapped her arms around me and sobbed into my shoulder, I felt as if I couldn't let her go. I pulled away and looked in her beautiful, crystal green eyes and for a moment, it was hard to believe that I'd hated her so much for everything she couldn't give me because of her illness, and right there in that moment, I would have given anything just to take what we did have with me through the departure gate. She felt so comfortable, so safe, and her eyes felt like my connection to both of those things that would in a moment be ripped away. How could I feel like that when for so much of my life I had felt such lack and such disappointment that she didn't stack up to the mum I had needed growing up? How could I feel so close to her in that moment, when for so much of my life she had felt so far away and so physically and emotionally distant? My whole life it felt like she was just out of reach, and the parts we could touch were just a confusing mix of hot and cold.

As I looked into Mum's eyes, I realised that in spite of everything, they were the eyes I could look for when I felt lost or afraid. It was just that, in so many moments when I was small, she'd been focusing in another direction.

They say that the eyes are the windows to the soul. The pupil of the eye is like an aperture on a camera, dilating or contracting, depending on the light; it's the lens through which we see our life. This channel is the one through which we see the beauty in the world or see everything there is to fear. The lens through which we see all the beauty in another human being or through which we see everything they lack and their faults. That lens guides our feelings, it guides how we act, and it guides what we decide in a moment that guides our experience in life. Perspective either gives us freedom or it takes it away.

In this moment of my life, at 21 years old, with my wild heart, I was choosing to see the opportunity of the world and experience freedom. I breathed that confirmation in, drew away from my mum and quipped, "Chile won't know what's hit them!" I hoped my smile would show how excited I was, but as I disappeared amongst the people and headed towards the gates that would lead me to my brand-new life, I was choking back my tears and I questioned turning around as I walked away.

It wasn't too late to ditch this whole idea and run back to safety … but something deeper than that brief conscious thought burned subconsciously. A desire I had always had to have an adventure and make a difference. I couldn't describe it. It was like listening to a rhythmic drumbeat that took my heart someplace else and into the most magical of daydreams.

Deep into the mountains where the mountain gorilla sits in all his majesty, protecting his land… Deep into the luscious green rainforest where indigenous families enjoy the magic of life amongst the sounds of the forest and none of the luxuries of modern life… Up and over miles and miles of sparkling ocean so deep that no one has ever reached its bottom to dusty little towns where slim and beautiful children with their eyes beaming and their shining teeth chase a football around in laughter and in joy…

A Soul Goal so deep and brought to life only in tiny pieces by random pictures and clips on the TV, but with an inner knowing anyway that these daydreams were always meant to be my reality. I felt a weird and ancient connection to South America and its indigenous culture. Like it was already part of me and the land was calling me home.

When I was a kid, I dreamed constantly about travel. I ripped pictures out of magazines and made plans to travel the whole world one day – someday – Someday Isle. I fantasised about what I now know is the life of a nomad. Travelling from place to place like the Littlest Hobo, "wherever I lay my head is home."

As school progressed, my dream took a more responsible turn, as we learned about careers and getting paid. I thought about becoming an Air Hostess because that way I could see the world and get paid. At college, as I acknowledged my passion to write (and my fear of flying), I refined my dream and pinned my hopes on becoming a BBC World journalist. Then, I went to university to study languages ultimately, not because I really wanted to go to university, but because I perceived it to be the best way to get a job that would give me the security my parents lost and to create success out the other side. I didn't want to take the risk of living through what my parents had. Security sounded good. It sounded safe, and maybe having a language would mean I could travel. And of course, university seemed like a "good crack."

I couldn't know if South America would be the fulfilment of my true Soul Goal, but I had to keep walking forward so I could find out. Arriving in Chile, I was not disappointed. It was a beautiful city, and after a while, I was settled, living with a couple of English girls, and I made friends. Don't get me wrong, at times it was hard, really hard. Everything was new to me, I often struggled with the language, and I missed home. Somehow though, I always muddled through, and after each struggle, things got easier and I felt stronger.

Towards the end of my first term of teaching at the university, I began to plan my summer break away. I wanted to see

Ecuador, Brazil, Peru, and Bolivia. I knew I wouldn't get around to them all, but planning as if I would made me so excited! I booked my bus for New Year's Day and tried to enjoy Christmas, but it was a funny time. Although I had met lots of people and the two girls that I lived with were lovely, I didn't really feel close to anybody, and suddenly, I really missed home.

While the sun shone bright in Chile, the sparkles of the tinsel on the trees in the streets made me think of the mounds of screwed up wrapping paper on the floor around our Christmas tree at home, Mum sweating over the oven (and burning the turkey!), and Dad asleep on the sofa. Christmas just didn't seem like Christmas in the sunshine with my friends and family so far away.

Christmas is celebrated on Christmas Eve in Chile. The families cook a big dinner and have drinks while the children are allowed to open their presents at midnight. One of the girls I lived with had been going out with a Chilean for a while, and he, too, was spending Christmas without his family, so we were invited to join him for dinner. He was a good man. We had met him during our first weekend in Chile, and he had made us feel welcome, and we instantly trusted him. That night was fantastic. We ate and drank far too much, and we exchanged little stockings that we had filled for one another under the Christmas tree. Mum rang me the following morning, we talked nostalgically about previous Christmases, and I chatted excitedly about my forthcoming trip. It felt like being apart from Mum, at university and on this trip, had helped our relationship to heal.

Christmas came and went, and before I knew it, I was on a bus heading off to the unknown—first stop north of Chile to see the Atacama Desert, then onto Peru where I would finally experience the Machu Picchu trail and see for real all the Inca history I had read about. From there, my plan was to head up to Ecuador and back down to Bolivia before heading home to Chile.

The trip was incredible. When I returned, I was both penniless and a very different person. My mind had grown, and my heart had expanded. I had become both a little more cautious and also way more confident because I had learned and experienced many things, some of them good, and some of them bad. It was a positive feeling because it felt good to feel like I had changed and grown as a person. More than anything, I felt content that I'd finally done something I'd always dreamed about and suddenly, I appreciated everything. It was also March by this time, and I felt so excited about going back to England in a few months to share all my tales!

There was one thing that worried me though as I boarded the bus from the Santiago airport back into the city and paid for it with my last few Chilean pesos. Before I had left Santiago in January, I had given up the tenancy in my flat, and so, officially, I had nowhere to return to. I kind of thought I'd figure it out while I was away, but that never really happened. I knew there were hostels I could stay in when I got back, however, now I was back in a city that had actually started to feel like home, so a hostel felt like a really uncomfortable idea. I had been travelling for weeks and weeks, and while that experience had been amazing, I hadn't seen the same face twice for three months. It suddenly felt refreshing to think about being back with the same people feeling safe, relaxed, and having a good time. So, in a spur of the moment, I decided to go back to the house where I had spent Christmas Eve. The girl I had lived with before the Christmas break was already there, and I was sure her boyfriend would help me out for a few nights while I waited for my pay cheque from the university where I worked and looked for somewhere new to live.

I got off the bus and dragged my (still massively overpacked) rucksack in the smog and the heat. March is a time of festivals in Chile—the end of summer, endless street parties and copious amounts of Pisco (the national drink) so on top of this, I had to fight my way down the street through hundreds of students celebrating, cheering, and dancing in the road. Sure enough though, as soon as I arrived, I was invited in with open arms. "Vuelve la Gringa!" (the white girl is back!) was my welcome—that was what they always called me because I struggled with my Spanish, and they laughed at how English I was.

Despite being exhausted from my journey, the next day I was persuaded to join my friend, her boyfriend, and some other friends on a road trip to the beach a couple of hours south. It was "El Paseo de Las Cruces"—a religious festival—and there was to be a huge party on the beach. I was excited.

The beach party was incredible, music and dancing all day long, sand, sun, sea, and an all-day barbecue! I took hundreds of pictures thinking how crazy the Chileans were and how I would laugh when I looked back at them! By dusk, I was tipsy and sleepy from the sun, and I decided to join the group of friends with my friend and her boyfriend, who were heading back to the flat where we were staying for a meal.

I remember the meal we had because I remember being thrilled at the fact it was the first time I had ever eaten fondue. Admittedly, there was a lot of wine on the table, but because I had drunk a few beers throughout the day, I just sipped a small glass of wine conservatively over the dinner and then felt awake again after I had eaten and rested. I was really keen to go out again when somebody suggested we head out to catch up with the celebrations in the town. From that point on though, my memories are hazy. I remember the club and the lights, and I remember someone buying me a drink, which I remember drinking only a little of, to be polite, and then I switched to water because I felt tired and wanted to be able to enjoy the night. From there, my memory is blank.

The next day I woke up in a bedroom. My head pounded, and I felt weird, sick, and confused. On the floor by the bed, one of the guys I remembered from the party the day before slept half naked, and I suddenly felt embarrassed and covered him up with my blanket as I passed by, trying to rack my brains to remember how we all got back that night.

Out in the lounge, others were rousing awake, and the sun poured in through the window was making me feel sick. I decided to go down to the garden where there was a pool and dangle my feet in the water. I sat for ages just staring into the water trying to think back, but all I could see was black, and my head throbbed, and I felt sore down below.

I felt so alone in that moment, and as I stared blankly, a tear dripped down my face into the water. Laughter disturbed me, and my friend joined me at the pool with a couple of girls I didn't recognize. Still drunk and rowdy, they giggled and poked me and teased me about "the state of me last night." I forced a dry laugh, and although I had no idea what they were talking about but my heart stopped in panic.

On the way back to Santiago in the car, I felt sick and I was fighting back painful gulps of tears. I hurt all over, and although everyone could tell something was wrong, when they asked me, I couldn't tell them what was wrong because I didn't really know, and part of me didn't really want to.

Back in Santiago, back with my friend and her boyfriend, I felt like there was nowhere to be alone. I just wanted to think and try to remember what had happened. Still, there were only blank memories, my pounding head, and now it felt like I had a urinary infection. I had visible bruises on the inside of my legs. Deep down, I knew what had happened even if I didn't know how. I was just too scared to admit it.

I had been raped. And maybe even drugged because how I felt was not like a hangover, and I couldn't remember anything, no matter how hard I tried.

Over the next few weeks, I had flashbacks about what had happened. I'd wake up seeing a dark silhouette and feeling a body ramming into me. I'd feel hands around my neck or across my mouth. I'd wake up with tears stinging my face and my heart racing, gasping for air.

I knew pretty soon after that night what had happened. I had enough pieces, if not the whole picture and the physical feelings, but I couldn't tell anyone because I didn't know what to say. And what if they thought I was lying because I didn't have all the details? I also felt this deep penetrating feeling like it was my fault anyway. Just like a child, I must have done something wrong, and so I had asked for what had happened. It was horrible. My mind was already writing the stories they would tell that would make more sense than my own.

Shortly after I arrived back in Santiago, I moved into a new flat and I became slowly more detached and distracted. The flashbacks became more frequent, and I couldn't sleep. Throughout my time in South America, I had kept a detailed diary, but through this time, when I undoubtedly needed to express the most, the pages of my diary were blank. I fell into a depression that I covered up quite well on the outside, but on the inside, I was crumbling. I stopped eating. I survived off two crackers and an apple each night for dinner and seeing the weight drop off me felt good. Like punishment.

Some days, I felt desperate, like I'd rather die than know what had happened. I wanted the thoughts that haunted me to go away because I couldn't rationalise them or find the truth of what had really happened. And socially, I just drank. I drank to ease the insecurity I felt and to do what everyone else was doing, hanging out and enjoying life.

When I look back at the photos I took of that day on the beach, I see my smile, and I find it hard to think that something so horrid happened just a few hours later, and that such innocent fun turned into such a nightmare that lived on until very recently. It was only a couple of years after I began to write this book, when I finally engaged in healing my trauma, that the flashbacks stopped. Until then, the dark shadow visited me regularly. I would feel his heavy weight on top of me pressing down and hurting me. I would hear my own voice crying, "No," and I would feel my tears running down my cheeks, sticking my hair to my face. I've even heard myself cry out the word "condom." The worst thing is that I don't even know if I said that or not. Whether it was my mind trying to make me feel better that I had at least tried to be responsible, or if in fact in that moment when I realised I couldn't get him off me, that this was my request. I don't know who it was that raped me. Everything was just shapes and feelings for such a long time with this punishing sense that what happened was not invited or right.

When you go through something like this, an experience that traumatised you, your body doesn't forget. Even if you are able let go of the mental shackles, the experience persists enough to be bound to you in your body. These body memories are quiet until an event, a sound, a sight, a touch, a word, or a person awakens them. After Chile, I even found eye contact impossible because it felt like whoever was looking at me might see enough of me that I would become vulnerable again, and they would take advantage of that.

ARMOURS.

These are the physical layers we place upon who we are authentically to protect us from the bad things we experience. We unconsciously create from the place of our trauma, and I invite you to see that trauma doesn't have to be big things that significantly change how you see yourself and the world. It can be small things like being laughed at in the school playground that leave deep scars and create an identity that is inauthentic and a perception that is inaccurate and damaging.

I did a trauma healing session once with a lady who'd had an experience at school where a bunch of girls had made a circle and not let her in. This fleeting experience had marked her deeply. In her business, she was having difficulty getting visible because in her body she was remembering being shunned by those girls. After our healing session, everything changed in a positive way.

Our identity and perception guides how we feel, and how we feel creates our circumstances through the actions we take and don't take. But how do we successfully shift our identity and perception, so that we can create everything we want and so that we stop running away from who we are authentically and our limitless potential. Our reactions and patterns are unconscious. This is what makes them so damaging; we literally don't know that we have them.

In 2009, I went for a procedure at a hospital that required me to be put under general anaesthetic. The experience was horrible because in the moment that I drifted out of consciousness, I felt like "it was happening again." I panicked, and I remember screaming on the inside for help, but the doctors never heard my words as the lights faded out. It was after this that my need for control got obsessive. I developed a chronic anxiety I couldn't break through, which became a curse on my life for the next 14 years.

I began to look at my life through a different lens. I stopped trusting people. I questioned their intentions and became hypervigilant. My brain became like a wired in, personal surveillance system on high alert, with the experiences that hurt me programmed in like case studies. My brain was deciding for me at all times what was safe or not. As this system alerted me more and more to the dangers in my world, my hope that the future might be better than the pain I was feeling on the inside diminished. I was becoming a slave to my emotions and my story and descending into darkness more and more.

When I came out of university, I immediately sought out a stable job and got myself on the career ladder within a solid company. The job had nothing to do with my university degree, nothing to do with what I actually liked, but it did have a good salary and good prospects.

I had a corporate position as a Sustainability Manager for a portfolio of shopping centres, and I felt out of my depth. I was hired because of my passion and my creative ideas to reduce the supermarket's environmental footprint. I was not qualified academically for it, so when I got the responsibility to do the job, I was afraid of getting it wrong. I felt like I was "winging it" and Googling to check whether my ideas were sound. Now, I understand that isn't the idea of creativity! Now, I know to ask where the ideas on google come from in the first place. They came from someone's imagination, someone who had the courage to act on them and believe in themselves.

I was afraid of being made to look stupid or not good enough for the job. And I feared the scarcity of losing the job. I had been promoted for the creativity and passion I had demonstrated in my original role, and yet I felt I had to be more than that to protect myself from being made to feel stupid and not good enough like I had felt so many times growing up.

By the age of 25, I was living in a whirlwind. Despite of my insecurity in my job, I was being promoted, winning awards, and sitting in high-powered meetings making big decisions, which to be honest I was still winging and still doing security checks on Google! Behind the scenes with the company car and the big cheque, I was burning out and feeling miserable. I was living away from my boyfriend, my friends and my family, and my self-esteem was being eaten away by bullying colleagues who seemed to be unhappy with my responsibility and fast success. Plus, the whole corporate value system of greed over hearts made me feel dirty.

I burned out. My experience in Chile started to creep out of the box I had thrust it in. For some reason, the lid I had slammed down hard wasn't holding anymore. My anxiety was getting worse, and I drank too much to make it all go away. I pulled away from my relationship and spent more time at my desk, working late, stressing out, trying to keep up the guise of the tenacious go-getter who wanted the career her parents never had with a stable income and success.

On the weekends, I was the life and soul of the party, pretending Monday was never going to come around again, but it always did. One day, I was making the three-hour trip like I always did on a Monday morning up to my office for another week in a hotel when the walls of my mind just caved in. Everything went black. My heart was beating hard in my chest, and I had no idea who I was anymore or what I wanted, and I suddenly couldn't bear another moment in my life. My life became an obstacle that was insurmountable.

I was thinking, it's so easy. I just pull the steering wheel and everything goes away. I was closing my eyes and feeling the pain just melt away and when I opened them, I had no idea how I was still alive. I found myself on the hard shoulder of the road with the cars whizzing by and sweat dripping down into my eyes. Then I realised it wasn't sweat, it was tears, and I couldn't stop crying.

That was the beginning of the end of my successful career.

We all, at some point, choose to walk down paths that aren't aligned with our true authentic self or Soul Goal. We do it to "fit in" or to fulfil others' expectations of us, or because we don't see other options at the time. We do it because we feel obligated to, or because we take on a role we think is right. We pile layers of life on top of instinct, purpose, and love for the things that make our souls dance. We exchange the things that make our hearts sing for the things that pay the bills and fulfil our life roles and the things that keep us safe.

At some point in life, we also experience hardships that change the way we view ourselves and how we view our world. Our perception and our perspective changes. We get more cautious. This gets celebrated as "growing up" and becoming an adult, and it certainly has its benefits as we avoid repeating silly mistakes and doing things that are not good for us or sensible. However, what if it is also a sign of the fire in our soul burning away and our dreams turning to ashes? What if our chosen direction is only the path we take because of silent fears that have caused our smart brain to default to limiting decisions so we don't experience "that" again?

Some of the things we do to escape our pain are bad things. They are just armour we put on to protect ourselves from feeling, experiencing, and succumbing again. I did some stupid things following what happened to me in Chile, like writing myself off with alcohol more times than I care to remember... just to forget.

Other things we do in response to our trauma end up making us silver linings. By this I mean we do them in reaction to our pain, but the decision ends up serving us.

This was me and Muay Thai Kickboxing. In 2009, when I was in the depths of anxiety, somebody suggested taking up exercise. I'd never been a fan of the gym. The monotony of the machines and routines bored the crap out of me. I had already written the idea off by the time I got in my car to drive home. And I didn't fancy going back to what I had always done, which was running. All of a sudden, I saw a sign on the side of the road for kickboxing. I felt like a lightning bolt struck me. That is what I would do, even though at the same time, the idea scared me to death. My mind was already made up. This was what I would do.

I will never forget the morning after my first session. I literally couldn't sit down on the toilet seat because my legs hurt so much! I had to hold onto each wall and lever my way down to the seat! And then lever my way back up again. But the pain felt... awesome! It took my mind off the anxiety in my chest. It gave me something else to focus on. I felt excited for the next class to improve on all the things I couldn't do in the first one. And it felt so good to kick the pads and physically get some of the frustration I felt with my life out. When I was exercising, I didn't feel anxious.

I think my life became a little better in that moment. Just by changing something in a way that had such a dramatic impact on how I was feeling at the time. And it was me showing up and me taking action that created the change, not something external to me. And that one decision to take that class created a ripple effect that led to where I am today.

At first, I admit I had the wrong intentions regarding the sport. It felt good to "lash out" and be the one overpowering someone else. In 2011, when we came to New Zealand and I joined a fight gym, I wanted to fight for reasons that were somewhere between anger and complete self-destruction. It felt good to fight. It even felt good to be the one who was beaten. There was something liberating in the physicality of it. I can't explain it. It's like I wanted the pain I felt on the inside to show up on the outside. So that the pain had some physical representation so that it might fade, like a bruise does, and finally go away. But nothing made the pain go away. I did feel powerful, though, even when I was the one who was being overpowered. I was still able to fight back because I had the use of my limbs unlike that night when my power was taken away.

I lost my first fight in an extravagant way. I got completely overwhelmed in flurry after flurry of punches and got my eye blacked up. I'd invited my husband's whole family to watch, and they have never come back and watched me fight since. They called it brutal and unnecessary and maybe they were right, but I was hooked, and in my mind, that fight was a win. Every day, in my fight against anxiety, I lost the battle to the fight or flight reaction of my nervous system, but in that ring, I controlled it. It gave me hope! If I could control my fear inside the ring, why couldn't I control it outside of the ring as well?

When we are in the midst of struggle, it is easy to feel overwhelmed, but ultimately it means we are in a victim consciousness where the struggle is happening to us. From within the struggle, a vision of something better is not something we can see, just like when I walked out of the food bank in 2017, and we were disempowered. But from my experience, and from my story, I know that it can be the simplest of things that can empower a significant shift in feeling that creates positive change.

In short, you don't need any of the bullshit you think you do to move forward from where you are now. I believe this is also true regarding all of the business planning tools, marketing courses, and other business support you are engaging... It won't work until you do the work... within yourself. Change is an identity shift. If the change you want to see in your life right now relates to the state of your finances, you likely have a "poverty or scarcity" identity, and you are likely in a victim consciousness. And if you truly want to move forward, you have to think of it like stepping through the eye of a needle, where there is no space for your limiting beliefs and stories to come with you. And as we have talked about, your intention to step forward in the vulnerability of taking all your armour off, must run soul deep....

It will be uncomfortable to shed what can't come through, but again, what I know is that heightened discomfort brings change into motion. This is **Awakened Wealth**, creating abundant choice by connecting you with your intention within at a soul level. If you choose this inner journey to change your life, the universe will put you into a pressure cooker and force you to shed what isn't aligned to the identity you want and your UNLEASHED vision. When I work to set this vision with my clients, we are not focusing on the "things" in my client's reality, we are focusing on "who" my client has become to create them. This is the first step of the *Quantum Leap Method*. Once we have begun to ignite the imagination with the details of this desire, we shift focus to connecting to an authentic expression of the client in their truth, away from their resistance and self-defeating patterns, which we replace with empowering beliefs through trauma healing so they can live consciously and in alignment with their Soul Goal.

Trauma Healing is the second step of the *Quantum Leap Method*.

You may wonder why the *Quantum Leap Method* doesn't start here, but I invite you to feel into your own situation to understand. Do you have resistance to making positive changes? A little like starting a gym membership in the New Year... you start off with the right intentions, you go for a few weeks and then you find yourself with a hundred great excuses not to go. You miss a few sessions and before you know it you are back to the bad habits you were trying to get away from. This is because of what I have already taught you about the brain... it does not like the unfamiliar. It will make you feel uncomfortable in moments of change, and it will create a state of inertia that takes you back to the reactions to life that come from your past that will never create the future you want.

To UNLEASH your Inner Millionaire and connect with a true identity that is soul-aligned and empowered, you have to smash your existing paradigm wide open. Our fear doesn't save us. It doesn't keep us safe like our evolution intended it to. It limits us, and it makes us miserable. I feared succeeding because of an unconscious limiting belief that success leads to inevitable loss. I'd seen my mum's sadness when my dad lost everything, and I had lived through my dad's feelings of failure. When I was about 16, I came home from school and found him nearly unconscious in my Mum and Dad's bed while Mum was out working and Nan occupied herself upstairs in her granny flat.

To this day, we don't know what he'd taken, but he told me later he wanted out that day. His failure felt heavy on me, and what both him and Mum were so afraid of, even though I never saw it or experienced it, it still terrified me. And yet, when I hit rock bottom that day in the food bank, what terrified me more was putting my own children through that fear. Through feeling like they weren't worthy of my love, of my full presence, or of everything I was put on this earth to give them. I saw how being shackled to my emotions and stress made me not present for them. I saw how "being busy, being busy" made me not responsive enough to them. And this killed me because this was exactly what I experienced as a child. In realising that and feeling the discomfort of it, everything began to change.

We cannot take ourselves into those uncomfortable places. Especially if we have a "trauma-organised nervous system"— one that goes into flight, fight, or freeze often. For years, because of this, I repeated the pattern of self-sabotaging my success until I learned about changing the way traumatic memories are stored in our body and brain, and until I understood there is an alternative to survival mode. If you are existing in a world right now where your unconscious fears are only allowing you to see the next thing in front of you—living pay check to pay check or even crisis to crisis—I welcome you to smash your existing paradigm wide open starting now!

It is not helpful for me to simply preach to you about how I managed to change everything because trauma does not heal from the top down. It is not helpful for me to share with you that you can be as "rich" with $10k a year as you would be with $100k a year because abundance is just a feeling, or tell you that you are good enough, that you have enough, that you are enough, and that you are whole, worthy, and lovable being just as you are in your imperfectly, wonderful human self.

You won't believe me until you heal from your past trauma, your story, from the bottom up. What I mean by that is that we heal from the inside out. We heal by leaning into our pain and not becoming it, which means we have to heal the trauma that organises our nervous system, and we have to be a willing passenger on that journey. A lot of people aren't. It's uncomfortable being confronted by the truth of your story, which is at the root of whatever struggle you have creating scarcity in your life.

Many will fool themselves that the scars of their story are healed, and while they may seem that way on the outside, on the inside, they are flesh that is rotting deep within. It creates a feeling like a void. You have tried to fill that void with love, wealth or some other material thing like I did... but like I experienced, the void doesn't go away.

THE VOID IS YOUR TRAUMA.

Healing trauma creates the belief and peace of mind that will enable you to connect with your intuition, unleash your creativity and reach the answers you need within that will help you take action and make positive changes.

The third step of the *Quantum Leap Method* is **aligned action and positive changes**, and nobody can make them for you. And nobody will be able to convince you to make changes you are not ready to make, which is why the *Quantum Leap Method* starts with connection to the truth of yourself, which wakes you up to how your core belief Blueprint—your internal operating system—is actually part of the survival skill you developed to survive in a world that let you down.

Your self-connection will wake you up to how you no longer need to believe that you deserved what you went through, so that the pain of it lessens and you have the sense of autonomy and control that makes you feel safe without the need for external validation that you are.

You will see how, if you are lacking love, you can heal and believe you are worthy of unconditional love without someone proving it to you from the outside. You will understand how you can make the identity shift that creates infinite possibility without waiting for the "right time" or "right circumstances" to let it happen. You will change physically, change your personality, and change how you accept less than you are worth because you no longer need to fill the void. You will understand how, when you were wronged by whoever hurt you, it was never about your worth or lovability, it was about whatever was going on in the life of the perpetrator, the pain in their heart and mind, and you will be able to send them healing and forgiveness. Your perception will completely change. And this will raise your frequency. Emotions of unconditional love and happiness will run through you. You will be detached from judgment and attached positively to the belief that you can't control life or the actions of the people around you, which will empower you to always be able to control how you respond to your life in your creative power. This is the fourth step of the *Quantum Leap Method*—shifted perception, living life on purpose and living in prosperity. You will awaken your Miracle Frequency. Life will start to be easier without you forcing the change of anything in your external reality.

And so, if you are working hard to shift your income right now… If you are sacrificing time with your children or your happiness or your health for your business… If you are working out of alignment with your Soul Goal because you fear scarcity, you can trust in my promise that you can stop.

PRACTICAL INTEGRATION

JOURNALING

Who were you before the experiences that created your silent fears?

What did you love to do?

Where did you play?

What did you play?

What were your favourite hobbies?

What did you want to be when you grow up?

Who did you want to become?

Do you remember the dreams and values you had before you knew of money and status?

I invite you to remember yourself in your authenticity.

Then I invite you to feel your desire and inclination to heal the void of yourself that your trauma created.

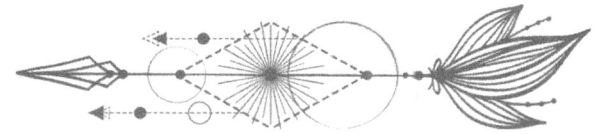

HEAL THE VOID YOUR TRAUMA HAS CREATED

"The rabbit hole went straight on like a tunnel for some way, and then dipped suddenly down, so suddenly that Alice had not a moment to think about stopping herself before she found herself falling down a very deep well."
LEWIS CARROLL

There have been three constants in my life. Writing, a love for the environment, and scarcity. In 2021, when I began trauma healing, I put scarcity to rest.

I'd considered ending my life because of a scarcity of hope.

I've cut corners and said no to opportunities because of a scarcity of money.

I've hidden myself away and given up trusting and taking people at face value because of a scarcity of safety.

However, all of these things were a perception, not a truth.

In 2021, Trauma Healing helped me to change my perspective and see things as they truly are. I began to move towards "full circle" with the intention I'd set in the food bank in 2017.

For years, I blamed the rape for my brokenness, but equally, for years I never dealt with it. It wasn't until I began the process of trauma healing that I realised the brokenness went back so much further back than the rape, and this was the beginning of the process of unravelling the feelings that were keeping me stuck.

When I trained to become a Life Coach in 2016, I'd had huge goals for this business, but my action did not level up. I would find myself regularly confused, overwhelmed, and unsure. The Life Coaching training helped me become aware of how much my life was out of alignment and helped me see how my most important value in life was freedom, but I'd lost the ability to be free at all. I was confined by the walls of my anxiety, anchored to the pain of my past, and absolutely unable to "just be." Inner peace was completely lacking for me, and I actively avoided any silence and solitude because in that space I connected with all the feelings I was working so hard to avoid.

Feelings don't go anywhere when we don't feel them. When we feel them, we transmute them. When we ignore them, we just press them down, bury them deep, and the energy of them is always fighting to rise. So, we busy ourselves to ignore that discomfort. Feeling the need to be busy all the time is a trauma response and a fear-based distraction from what you'd be forced to acknowledge and feel if you slowed down. I always had to be doing something because silence was a frightening place to be. I couldn't take time to "just be" because I couldn't connect with the feeling of my pain rising, and I wasn't at peace with who I was. However, instead of changing something back then, I instead felt confronted by the fact that everything in my life at that time represented the opposite to the truth I was discovering about myself. I wasn't ready to make the decision to give up the safety of where I was, despite how uncomfortable I was living a life that didn't fit my Soul Goal. I tried to launch my Life Coaching business, but it was a flop. I know now that I was fighting for it to flop. This was my unconscious directive because I feared everything I couldn't control, feared uncertainty, and I didn't believe I was capable of creating or maintaining the success I'd never had.

Is there's an area of your life that you really want to grow in, a Soul Goal you have and want to realise? It is how you feel that is holding you back, right? Sure, there is a gap between what you have compared to what you want, but ultimately the idea of changing something that might lead to a change in your reality feels more uncomfortable than the discomfort of staying where you are. Experiencing whatever is keeping you stuck with feelings is protecting you from what you fear because the feelings will make sure you stay stuck. You are frozen in the fall from whatever branch snapped for you and shattered your illusion of security to pursue the call in your Soul Goal.

Alberto Villodo, in his book, *The Heart of The Shaman*, calls this our "Sacred Dream." And he shares that

"You find your sacred dream by transforming three common dreams many of us are convinced are true and cannot seem

to wake up from. They are the dream of security, the dream of permanence, and the dream of love that is unconditional. When you transform these dreams—when you accept that life is ever changing, that your mortality is a given, and that no one can liberate you from a life of fear and insecurity except you—the chaos in your life turns to order and beauty prevails. When you find your sacred dream, the creative power of the universe, known by the shamans as the Primordial Light, becomes available to you to create beauty in the world and to heal yourself and others. You become a luminous warrior."

...But you, my beautiful reader, and past version of myself, are unconsciously choosing a life that will never unleash your Soul Goal and create the income and impact that you want.

An important thing to know is that there is a reason you are having the feelings you have, and there's a reason that you're not doing anything about them. Your feelings are a safety net to the vulnerability you are scared to experience because you haven't discovered your creative power yet. Discovering this is a prerequisite to your Miracle Frequency awakening, so you can have it all, and it can be easy. And it is a tragedy you haven't cracked this Abundance Code already! My parents are close to their 80s, and I believe that they still haven't discovered that they have creative power yet! I believe they will go to their graves miserable because their hearts are full of trauma that they never got a chance to heal, and because of that, they have made an unconscious choice not to see the beauty and magic of life. They just see all the bad shit instead.

"HOPE"

H.O.P.E... Hold On, Pain Ends.

Your past is your greatest power in creating the future you want. Because your learnings become the reason you reveal your own creative power, and you start creating and attracting a new level of abundance in your life.

When I began writing this book at the end of 2018, I never actually meant to write a book. I was just trying to take the load that was sitting on my heart away. As I began to write, I started to see all the different parts of my personal story that had created my armour in a way I hadn't seen them before. And it began to change how I felt.

Imagine your armour as heavy metal chainmail that you are wearing, which is weighing you down and making you walk awkwardly through life. You feel the weight of this armour. You know you are not showing up in your true, authentic power. You feel there is more to your life, and you are craving freedom from the hell you are in. Freedom is the ability to radically express your authentic truth. So, if you truly want freedom, if you do have a Soul Goal, and you are ready to stop pushing it to "SomeDay Isle" and take massive action, it's time for you to take your armour off. You start by stripping away your limiting beliefs and healing your trauma to bring you back to truth. Your truth is how you will make the difference you want to in your life and in the lives of others.

I know you have done mindset work in the past, but it hasn't worked because your problem sits in your subconscious mind and your unconscious body. Mindset work is conscious. This book is about true healing. Healing all the energy of your past story that sits in your subconscious mind and unconscious body because while you are still programmed by that same energy, you're always going to live out the same patterns. It's time to consciously choose who you want to become, and it's time to consciously choose the emotions that will empower you to live a life that reflects your true desires and true Soul Goal within.

You can condition yourself to feel good most of the time and understand how you shift your limiting emotions to be able to thrive, even in the hardest of times. That said... I think you'll find the hard times are less frequent when you begin to exist in a whole new energy, a higher vibration that starts to attract more of what you want and less of what you don't want. After I wrote the first draft of my book, I began to call myself a #RecoveredSurvivor because I realised that we wear "surviving" like a badge of honour. "I survived that hardship," we say. "I survived that abusive relationship." "I survived that bullying." But if you're still surviving, you're still feeling all the emotion of everything you have been through and those feelings are blocking you from creating everything you want.

It's when you can tell your story without emotion that you are no longer attached to the story that scarred you, and you are in your most powerful state to create change.

I had a client once who described healing her trauma like finally being able to look at a picture book and only see pictures, instead of feeling all the emotions of the storyline. She finally felt emotionally free from her pain and able to share from the wisdom of her experiences. The brain works in mental pictures just like a picture book, so we can go back into those mental pictures and see things from a totally new perspective, just like I started to as I wrote the first draft of this book. Changing perspective is the way we can change the emotions that we feel and the meaning we have held onto, which changes how we show up and take action in our lives.

At any moment, you can be in control of how you feel.

Which means.... You can't change the world, you can't change your partner, you can't change your boss, or your pay check or all the bad things that keep happening to you. And you don't need to. Because you can change how you feel, and if you change how you feel, you will change your frequency and your reality will change without you doing anything at all.

This does not mean you will always have good feelings or never feel a bad feeling again, but you will always be able to move your emotions—shift your state—in the moment and get back to productivity and creativity with more ease. I will show you exactly how to do this and give you a free resource in the third part of this book. As a changemaker, what does this mean for positive change in the world? It's exciting, right? All these problems we are trying to solve, all these charities we are trying to fund to solve the problems that seem never to end, what if we could make it all go away just by healing ourselves?

It has been proven that we can. It is known as the **Maharishi Effect.**

You may have heard about it. There are 43 published or presented papers reporting on the results of it across the world. What the studies PROVE is that there is a long-range field effect of consciousness. Groups across the world have come together in transcendental meditation and it has improved societal trends. The first published study found that when small cities reach 1% of their population instructed in the **Transcendental Meditation** technique, they showed a reduced rate of FBI Part 1 crimes for the next year and a decreasing trend the following years, compared with matched control cities. This is literally scientific PROOF of how you can change all the problems you want to change in your life by doing nothing at all.

Your emotions are energy in emotion. You have to feel them to move them, and they carry beautiful messages for you. They are telling you what you need in the moment to get into the state that's going to create the experience of living that you want. But your inner thoughts, feelings, and words are like the rabbit hole in the opening quote of this chapter by Lewis Carroll if we do not control them. If something terrible happens, and we don't deal with it in the moment, learn its lessons, and let it go, the experience weighs us down and prevents us from success. Our energy is the vibration we put out into the universe, and the universe reflects that energy right back at us in our abundance. Our external abundance mirrors our internal abundance. There is a beautiful, constant giving and receiving flow of energy in our universe unless we block it with the limiting thoughts that we have.

The feelings that being raped created—shame, fear, guilt—were thoughts that limited me for years. I used it as an excuse not to look inward because I'd locked the bad memories away in a box deep within my mind, and opening that box made me feel all the shame of it. And I felt shame for not being able to get over it. So, I carried on with life like it never happened. The problem is, the monsters in the box didn't go anywhere, and their power over me grew as they expanded. These evil claws began to poke through the cracks of the box and threaten to consume me from the inside out. So, how could I ever experience abundance externally when my inside was so messed up. And how can you?

TRUTH BOMB.

It is not that you "can't afford it" or you "don't have time" or that you are "not supported enough" or "unlucky." It's not the drama you are focused on right now that feels overwhelming that's blocking you from making money. It's that somewhere, at some point in your life, something happened to you that gave you the belief you are not worth the effort, or the effort is not worth it, or you'll fail if you try...

When I was in the UK, I blamed my environment. I blamed my parents. I blamed my brother. I blamed my job. I blamed my friends. And so, in 2011, like I've already mentioned, I packed up my whole life and migrated to New Zealand where I could start afresh. Guess what I figured out... Our environment doesn't change who we are, and it's who we are that dictates how we respond to the stuff that happens in our lives! So, there was every risk that when I arrived here in New Zealand, I would just repeat the same patterns because our actions are determined by the deep conditioning of our past.

Think about your past right now. Every time someone called you stupid, you filed it away with meaning attached. Every time you felt worthless, you filed it away with meaning attached. Every time you felt ugly, you stored it away with meaning attached. Just like I already taught you, before we are eight years old, we have already built a solid foundation of our belief based on all the "programming" we have had from the people in our lives, the television shows we have watched, and the experiences we have had.

I coached a client once who was having considerable self-worth issues. She wanted to start writing a blog as a business, but she was procrastinating and holding back taking action.

I asked her what she wanted to blog about, and she shared that she had this big passion for vegan food and helping others to eat a vegan diet to stay healthy and slim. I questioned her about what this looked like to her—her perception of healthy and slim—and she described somebody very different from herself. The perfect body she'd never had and had always strived for.

As we dug back into her past, she connected with a memory that she acknowledged she would never have attached to the issues she was currently having about her body image without some coaching. She remembered always feeling like she had a different/subordinate body to other people. She had struggled with her own weight and body happiness throughout her childhood and adulthood. I asked her where she thought she got the idea that a perfect body weight/body shape even existed, and she said that, early on, it would have been her Barbie dolls and, as she grew a little older, it would have been women on TV shows and magazine covers.

Think about that conditioning for a minute. Think about the power of it and how it has directed her whole life of feeling overweight and unattractive. What we focus on, we attract. Towards the end of our session, I asked her to imagine five healthy women with similar healthy body weight in a line, but they were all different in other ways such as hair, height, etc. I asked her how she would pick out the one who had the perfect body. And the light bulb went on. She couldn't. She said, there is no perfect body, everybody is different. And right there, in that moment, she rewired her brain.

Until we "rewire" our subconscious programming, we will repeat the unconscious patterns directed by our conditioning and experiences. Before I understood this, my pattern was to ditch everything and run away from what was making me uncomfortable because of the unconscious patterns I had. The decision to ditch everything and long-haul it to New Zealand probably was over-exaggerated, but it has ultimately been the best decision I ever made.

Granted, my struggle came with me in my mind because of my focus, but then I also went cold turkey from the intense drama I had left in the UK. I met new people, I got married, and had new experiences. And I started noticing the humility of New Zealand people in general. I kept hearing the words, "It is what it is." I'll never forget how curious I was about the fact that people could just let stuff go like that, and I loved the value of family and time spent just hanging outside or at the beach bash.

I began to learn a whole new way of life where I began to value more of what I had in my life, rather than worry and fret over what I didn't have. New Zealand fits me like a glove. Yes, my struggle came with me to live here. Yes, I also brought my learned behaviours and beliefs, so I did default back to the same sort of jobs I did in the UK for a while, and I felt the discomfort of them not fitting the person I truly am, again. But finally, my move to New Zealand began to break my habits of a lifetime.

BREAKING YOUR HABIT OF A LIFETIME

After I bought into the wearable technology company in 2017, I began to grow my own team of distributors. I started to see how one of the biggest blocks for the other people wanting to wear and share the tech was a fear of rejection, which was presenting as a lack of motivation to reach out to the people that would build their businesses. From whatever experience they'd had in the past, where they had experienced the pain of rejection, they were feeling the anticipation of this pain as they were trying to reach out on direct messenger to people and make connections that might lead to sales.

When we feel the anticipation of a past pain in this way, our brain will scream excuses at us not to do the work, to go do something else, cross a different task off the to do list, or scroll on a little further through Facebook to find the person that will definitely say yes to looking at our proposal. This leads to the procrastination and lack of productivity that sabotages our business results.

I see this happening with my coaching clients. Fear is literally the anticipation of pain at a biological level. At some point, somewhere, they have felt the pain of rejection, and their brain is doing its #1 job, which is to protect effectively. We don't even realise this process of protection is happening. It's unconscious, which is why we have to make a conscious decision to focus on everything we are working for and attach ourselves to the power, drive, and pleasure of that outcome instead. The goal is to ensure that the pain of a rejection that might never happen doesn't sabotage the action that will create results.

Another amazing mentor I had, again through the tech company, used to say that our beliefs drive our enthusiasm, which drives our action, which drives our results. He used the acronym, "B.E.A.R." to represent this: **Beliefs - Enthusiasm - Action - Results**, and I have found this so powerful that I brought the principle into my Coaching Certification. Basically, if you haven't gotten the results you are seeking in life, take a long hard look at your beliefs.

When I was raped, I think I unconsciously believed I'd lost my choice to be safe in life because the power of my decision got taken away from me that one night. I gave into the helplessness of that feeling, and I lost my strength to fight to get it back for a while. And yet, I am here today because I got that fight back. There is always life on the other side of the pain. We can always let go of it.

Bring a picture up right now in your mind's eye of you when you were a child. Imagine you have a paintbrush in your hand and a big piece of blank paper on the table in front of you. What are you going to do? Don't look through the eyes of your adult self... look through the wonder of the eyes of your child self. What would you do? You would slosh the paint and colour all over the paper with complete freedom, right? And you would see your creation as beautiful because it presents a reality to you, as you see it in complete freedom from the barriers of perfection or limited thoughts.

When you are a child in that innocence, what you imagine is what is. Until something or someone smashes that paradigm and imprints a new belief. Now we are getting to the crux of things. Are you starting to see how you have the power to change your reality by changing your thoughts and how your thoughts are sabotaging you? Your thoughts come from your feelings. They are impulses from your nervous system that has been programmed by the memories of the pain you experienced via the commands imprinted into your brainstem that directs the messages to your nervous system so that it knows how to keep you alive.

You are in a **Survival Mode** that has you imprisoned in your Survival Mind when we exist in our truth in our hearts.

We can be powerful creators of our lives and create the futures we want for ourselves if we are connected to who we truly are in our hearts, are clear on what we truly want and if we make the decision to be in control of our mind and our focus. You can learn how to do exactly that. You don't have to be a victim to your biology, trauma and programmed habits of a lifetime. You can break them. However, most people prefer to remain comfortably miserable. What I mean by that is that it's comfortable staying where you are, even though you know deep down that it is not where you want to be, and this lack of alignment with your true desires manifests as emotions like frustration and resentment, feelings of anxiety and depression, and maybe even bitterness or unkindness towards others.

When my Coach, Lesley, helped me question my beliefs, I had freedom to explore the new habits I could integrate that better aligned to the life and experiences I wanted to create. I believe I manifested her with the energy of my intention to change my life. I believe I manifested the pressure cooker of the uncomfortable working situation I had in my corporate job in Manchester too. I asked to be liberated from that situation, and I was. This breakdown was a breakthrough to a more aligned life.

Take a moment to reflect on your own life. Is your experience a mirror of your energy? Is the situation you have really a bad thing if you look at the vision you have of the life that you want? Are things really falling apart or are they aligning? Coaching with Lesley was the first time in a very long time that I was forced to stop and reflect on questions like these. I was able to question whether my beliefs were actually mine or whether they were beliefs that had been imposed on me, either by society, my parents or the media, or whether they were born out of my past experiences, and I began to change my perspective on the meaning of those experiences, and I started to feel a whole lot different about myself and my life.

In 2018, the year after meeting Lesley, and after writing the first draft of this book and beginning my personal development journey, I saw how I had lived a huge portion of my life in my **Poverty Identity**. I went "gung-ho" with personal development and the shift this created in my life was powerful. However, I still felt like I had this gaping hole inside. This void I could not fill with anything, just like I had working in my corporate job in Manchester, which had given me good prospects and a stable income, but only ever really left me feeling EMPTINESS. It would always feel like something was missing, so I would crash and burn and run to the next thing that might fill the void up. Even having my two beautiful children didn't "resolve" it. This was a damaging pattern.

"I WANT MY LIFE TO BE DIFFERENT."

It was 2021, and I was sobbing into my knees, hidden away in my bedroom, and those words were resounding around and around in my head. The guilt cut like a knife because for an outsider looking in, I had everything a girl could want with a husband, three kids (now), a house, cat and dog, and security.

It felt like the life I had been living for nearly 40 years had violently spat me out. The journey I had taken to get to know myself outside of my stories and conditioning, my values, what was important, and what I truly deserved had taken off my rose-tinted glasses that I didn't realise I had on, and there was no stepping back into the Matrix.

My life had become uncomfortable.

My letting go of conformity had started rubbing a friction against those around me and what had always made sense in so many areas of my life didn't make any sense anymore, and I was becoming more marginalised from society. It didn't help that, at this point, the Covid pandemic was happening and I did not believe one single ounce in the vaccines that were brought in to save us. I was questioning everything and the relationship with my husband started to really be strained.

Just to add insult to injury, New Zealand's lockdowns and controls regarding Covid meant that by not being vaccinated, I couldn't be in most public places. The unvaccinated were outcasted. My husband and I became two opposing sides of an argument, and it was horrible. We argued when we have never argued before, but then, in previous years, I had never allowed myself to have a voice.

I started to feel desperately lonely and yet the most self-assured I had ever been at the same time. My UNLEASHED vision was so clear, and even though I didn't know how to make it my reality yet, I had this illogical peacefulness about that.

I was sobbing into my knees because I realised that everything had changed, but only within myself, and I suddenly felt scared about my external reality changing to match. I was afraid I would lose my husband completely because he wouldn't accept this new version of me. He had met me and fallen in love with me when I was broken, and the dynamic of our relationship was that he protected me. I didn't need that protection now, and it felt scary that there was no guarantee he would continue to love me now that I was fixed.

When I was broken, I didn't know my needs, and I didn't have a voice. I only knew how to survive. I was a prisoner to my beliefs, and we can't expect more out of life than we believe about it, like we can't expect more out of ourselves than we believe about ourselves. What I'd always been lacking was nothing other than BELIEF. There was no scarcity of anything else. Scarcity is an illusion that stops us from seeing the vision of the life we want. Our trauma makes us fear setting an UNLEASHED vision, and our limiting feelings allow us to settle for survival mode instead of living into our creative power.

Before I healed, just like my parents, I didn't understand the Miracle of the Universe to make everything that we want available to us just by focusing on it and aligning our energy to match it instead of focusing on what is lacking.

However, the difference between me and my parents was that my broken promise to my girls and my broken promise to give them the world was enough to get me to change my perspective that I was powerless in a world that I'd believed for too long was scary and horrible.

This wasn't the truth, but believing that had held my creative power back. It had made me surrender to the belief that I am not enough. It had made me focus so hard on protecting my children from everything that I was so scared about that I didn't know what my potential was outside of them.

So, in place of the focus on a vision of my happy and fulfilled life for them, I had my focus fixed on how I was going to pay the next bill or cover the food shopping trip and keep them safe. My focus was fixed on busying myself to ignore my stress, my guilt and the hardship of our situation—my struggle and scarcity. And guess what? I was manifesting more of that in my life. My mindset equalled my vibration, which matched the low level of success in my life.

Stop and ask yourself a serious question right now. Whatever you feel—do you want to get to this time next year and still be feeling it?

Because that's the truth. Your comfort zone might be comfy, but if staying comfy is leaving you feeling uninspired, emotionally affected, and stuck, then that is comfortably miserable. And it's nothing to be ashamed of to admit you're stuck there. I was. Way before our financial walls ever caved in, I had avoided stretching myself and doing something different because doing that felt more uncomfortable than the discomfort of staying where I was. Does that make sense?

In 2021, when I finally began to invest in trauma healing, I had a profound awakening regarding my unhealthy pattern of seeking safety. In a subconscious reprogramming session, my mind guided me back to the memory of my nan's bedroom. After my nan had moved in with us when I was a child, she had become a significant impact on my life. She had always made me feel safe and grounded and was always my symbol of strength and the antithesis to how my mum never really saw the sunny side of life. My nan smiled on the rainy days and always found the silver lining to the clouds that were grey. She got excited about the simple things and showed gratitude in ways I am only just learning to do now.

It was like she had some magic influence over my world, and it was less scary whenever she was around although she was very strict. She never took any rubbish from me and my brother, but I respected her for that. I will never forget the day I decided to try and have a text conversation through the television with a boy I had met. Have you ever done that? I can't remember how it worked, but you could connect by text and use a channel on the television. It was the first time ever that I had gotten flirty with a boy. Kinda sexy actually! And then my nan barged into the lounge red-faced and told me to turn off my trash and wash my mouth out with soap! Little did I know she'd been settled in watching *Emmerdale* or *Coronation Street* or something in her granny flat upstairs, and I had turned the channel over from downstairs to do my dirty deed. She'd read all of it as I typed. I couldn't look her in the eyes for weeks! I was mortified!!!

In the house moves that were caused by the loss of my dad's business, my nan was "home." In the confusion of growing into my teenage years with my dad mostly absent while he figured out his own stuff, she was "sense." She was wise, and she was inspirational. Instead of getting old like most grandmas do, she continued working and wore bright-coloured power suits and bold lipstick. When my dad moved back from Birmingham after he'd tried to save our old house and struggled with the teenager he was confronted with that he hadn't seen transform from the child he left, she was my warmth and understanding. In short, she was my world.

While her physical health did deteriorate over a few years, it seemed her mindset stayed extremely strong until right at the very end when what felt like out of the blue, she let go. She let go of being strong and made it very clear she was ready to go; she was tired and over the pain of fighting. I rushed home from my job in Manchester, and I sat with her every hour as she slipped into unconsciousness. I sang to her, and we played her favourite songs as I held her old, frail hand.

Late one evening, Mum encouraged me to go home. She said I needed to get some rest and that it was okay because she and Dad would be there to sit with her. Dad said, when he told me she had gone, that he and Mum had sat together with her for hours until Mum couldn't cross her legs any longer and went to the toilet. It was just my nan and my dad alone, and then she slipped away. It was like she waited until the only person who could deal the easiest with her parting was there, like even in those very last moments, she was thinking of us and protecting us from seeing her slip away from this time and place.

James Blunt's song, *Carry Me Home* says:

> *"As strong as you were, tender you go*
> *I'm watching you breathing for the last time*
> *A song for your heart, but when it is quiet*
> *I know what it means and I'll carry you home*
> *I'll carry you home."*

My dad told me that when he heard this song it resonated with this silent pact my nan had made with him, like she trusted him to hold her space in those final moments and be the place between her and the impact her loss would have on me and my mum, to be the messenger of the sad news in the hopes it would land more softly than hearing her last breaths.

That moment broke my dad. In all my selfishness of youth, I had never seen how much my nan also meant to him. They had built a friendship that went much further than just being her son-in-law or my mum's husband. He had cared for her, just like he had cared for my mum in all those moments where she couldn't care for herself. And he had done this, both with my mum's support and without it, as she had needed caring for also. In this realisation, my dad became my hero. And when I hear that song, my heart hurts for what we lost in my nan, and I feel the grace that was my grandmother all over again.

After I lost my nan in 2009, I started searching online for projects to volunteer for abroad, and I came across a little organisation in Brazil called Iracambi. Their website was homemade and basic. The information was overwhelming so, I reached out by email and shared that I wanted to help. A girl called Jemma wrote back to me and, in what felt like only moments, an old Soul Goal that I'd laid to rest after Chile came alive again. She promised to send me an application form, and for the first time since my nan's last breath, I felt like I could breathe.

I sent back the application form, and things moved very quickly. I had to put together a case to my employer for a working sabbatical. I committed to making the trip a learning experience, to come back with ideas and best practice in sustainability, looking at things from another perspective in a country where its progression was (and still is) imperative. I wanted to research and learn about how my company could take more responsibility for sustainability.

I even had a vision of setting up a partnership between the main shopping centre I managed in Manchester and a *Golden Lion Tamarin* charity in the South East of Brazil, so that the staff in our centre could understand better why we ask them to turn out lights, switch off computers and recycle. Maybe if they could connect the impact of these simple things to the reality of the rainforest's degradation and the plight of the tamarind, it would educate them in a way that would open their eyes and close the loop in more responsible action. I also intended to visit charities and businesses in the three main cities and learn not only about the potential impact my company had upon Brazil, but also investigate how we could help Brazil in their goals and offer other income options to those cutting down the rainforest.

I remember taking the journey to Brazil like it happened yesterday. And just like when I had gone to Chile, I was terrified.

I arrived in the chaos of the Rio airport at midday and found the bus that I needed to travel on wasn't leaving until 6 p.m. I was faced with a horrifying conundrum... wait the six hours I needed to for the bus at 6, or fight my way back through the carnage of the bus stop and airport to find some accommodation in Rio overnight.

At this point in my life, my anxiety in crowds of people was unbearable, and there were literally people, cars, motorbikes, and buses everywhere! I also had no idea how to navigate myself to somewhere to stay in Rio (and I hadn't researched it beforehand, having pinned my hopes on there being a bus to Muraie.) My resolve, after much pondering and walking through the crowds of people in circles with all my luggage on my back, was to head back to the ticket guy I had told that I didn't want a ticket for the bus to tell him that I actually did want a ticket for the bus. He was, thankfully, a very nice gentleman, so I needn't have been so weary about reapproaching him. He was very patient considering he didn't speak any English, and my Portuguese was proving to be awful!

The highway, as I finally got on my way, unwound into the stunning scenery for which Rio is famous. To the left of me was the sea, and I remember that a big bird (could have been a heron or something similar) had taken flight at the same height of my window, just a little way away from me, and it felt like we were moving together in the sunshine.

The sun was beating down, and the water sparkled. The heat was intense. To the right of my bus lay the favelas (or the shanty towns as they are more famously known). I'd studied a bit of Portuguese before I'd arrived, and the teacher had shared articles on what living in the favelas was like. They looked just like any other neighbourhood where children played in the street, adults walked with grocery bags, and teenagers flirted over a Coca-Cola in the sunshine.

It was hard to imagine the crime and poverty described within the articles or if you have watched the movie, City of God but the appearance of the favelas was astonishing. Like every available brick, slate and colour had been used just to be able to make a home, while in contrast, the city of Rio appeared affluent. There was something about this that resonated with me—choosing somewhere to be that ultimately meant living in poverty, sort of like how my parents had struggled and hustled to live where we did as children with the posh school and posh house.

The heavens opened as my bus finally rolled out of the city, and the most incredible lightning storm ensued. The lighting strikes were so defined and precise that I was scared the bus would get hit, but as the rain pelted down and the sun began to set, I began to calm down and settle back in my seat. I was starting to relax and enjoy the journey.

I arrived in Muraie at just before midnight and thankfully found a hotel to stay in right opposite the bus station. I'd worried myself silly throughout the entire five-and-a-half-hour trip that there would be nowhere to stay and I'd have to sleep on the bus station floor.

Exhausted, sweaty, and uncomfortable, I couldn't under-stand (or didn't have the patience to try and understand) the poor guy who tried to help me behind the reception desk. I remember panicking as I wandered up the stairs with my keys about what the bill would be in the morning; for all I knew he'd sold me the penthouse. I reasoned that, in truth, after the 15-hour plane ride, six hours on the bus station floor, and almost another six hours on the bus, I wasn't sure I cared. I showered, covered myself in insect repellent, then settled myself into bed to eat the complimentary crisps and drink the miniature can of Skol lager that washed down a handful of vitamin tablets, just to balance things out. It was so hot that my back stuck straight to the pillow! I was looking forward to what the onward journey would bring the next day, but I just felt so worried about everything. Just one more bus and a taxi to go, I hoped.

I was so anxious those first few days in Iracambi about the pro-ject I was volunteering for. I was hyper-alert as if everything was dangerous. Granted, I was in the middle of the rainforest, and I remember reasoning to myself that "it would be hard not to be afraid" with the spiders, the snakes, and the isolation. And yet, I was afraid like this back at home every day in my daily life. This was just me. Always on edge. Always worrying. Always waiting for the worst to happen. What's that known as? Catastrophic thinking? I went to Brazil to see about car-ing for the environment from another perspective, but I came home with another perspective of myself. Living my life terri-fied was the habit of a lifetime that I was ready to break.

Iracambi was like a spiritual experience. The forest healed me, and its life enlightened and inspired me. For years, I was so focused on getting to the top of the corporate ladder that I forgot everything else (and everybody else) in my life. I know now that this method of immersion was just a distraction from the pain I felt in my heart. In Iracambi, I realised I didn't want to be that way anymore. I wanted my life back. I didn't want the big cheque. I wanted a little garden that I could sit in at the end of the day. I wanted to come home to somebody at the end of the day. More than anything I wanted to shine again. My light had gone out.

As I worked each day, whether in the nursery replanting little trees or in the little lab on the computers, a little hummingbird visited me. I fooled myself into believing that it was the same bird each time because it always chose a time when no one else was around, and I smiled so hard when it did! I'd watch it hover in the air and glance at me before it skittered away.

I'd lost this ability to be mindful with the onset of the anxiety that plagued me. If I stopped for any length of time, the feeling of anxiety flooded in. Mornings were terrible. As soon as I opened my eyes and became conscious of a new day, I was anxious again. However, here, something was different, and I was finding the joy of peacefulness and what I now recognize was gratitude. I was fond of spotting "Tac," the lizard that lived in my nursery compost heap. Even though he was big and intimidating, he became less scary as the days went on. We learned to co-exist. He would creep out of the long grass, hunting for eggshells, fallen leaves, and flowers in the nursery as the wind gently rustled the trees. This calm was as invigorating as the tepid rain that pounded down on my shoulders and soaked my clothes and hair right through most days.

One day, a rainbow appeared right in front of me. Its intense colour burnt right through my soul, and I suddenly saw clearly. I had been so ashamed of being who I really am because "that girl" felt like such a burden as a child, only worth attention that was bad attention from my mum and dad. "That girl" felt stupid and uncool at school. And in Chile "that girl" got raped. "That girl" had stupid dreams her whole life that went "against the grain," but right there in that forest, "that girl" was the only person I wanted to be.

One day in the forest as the rain beat down, I made my first full-bodied intention to "change everything" when I got home from my trip. Maybe if I had stuck to this intention, that day in the food bank may never have happened....

The rain was absolutely pouring, and one of the pipes in our water system was blocked with something. I was working alone that day because the guy I normally worked with was sick. I was asked if I knew the way confidently enough to the water pipes, and I just nodded and said yes. Turns out I didn't. As I walked in the rain, hacking a path through the forest, everywhere began to look the same. I couldn't find the pipe, and I couldn't find my way back to where I had started either. After what felt like ages, I walked into this little clearing, and I stopped, struck by a stabbing realisation in my heart. Nothing at home matched the feeling of this! Here I was, lost in the forest, with mud and rain up to my waist and I felt complete FREEDOM. I dropped to my knees with my hands in the air. I couldn't tell if I was crying or laughing or both. And I promised myself, "I am going to change everything."

As I travelled on my itinerary through Brazil, looking for answers to my company's questions, I found more and more answers to my own—how I wanted to live my life, what was actually possible, and how I could answer my soul goal to make a difference.

At one point in the trip, I met up with a friend who I had shared a flat with after the rape in Chile. I never told him what had happened, but I know he knew something was wrong. He was very protective of me and loving during our time together. As I hid myself away in my room, he would knock on the door and sing to me. He made me a bunch of flowers out of the end of guitar strings. He asked if I was okay all the time. I allowed him to care, and we grew very close, like brother and sister.

I was overjoyed when he said he would come and meet me in Brazil, but on the trip, we argued. He told me he didn't recognize me and that I was angry. He said, "Clara, you cannot save the world!" And I yelled back saying that I didn't want to, I just wanted to do my part and preserve what is so precious and that this was not wrong or unrealistic. But I wasn't telling the truth. I did want to save the world. And he was right, I was angry. But I told him that I was just tired and sad about my nan, who he told me I had to let go.

Let go?

This made me angrier but I wasn't angry at him. I was angry at my nan for letting go of me and leaving me to deal with everything without her. She had always been my safe place. My constant. The hand to hold in the turbulence of my mum. When she held my hand, it didn't matter that it felt like the ground was falling away beneath me. How could she have given up?

I had carried this anger for so long. I think I felt angrier at her than at the boy who had raped me because I couldn't face the reality of him. I couldn't face the reality of the rape at all. I felt ashamed that it had damaged me in the way it did. Other people go through so much worse. Why couldn't I just get over it? That made me feel ashamed of myself too. It was easier to pretend that it never happened.

Upon my return from Brazil, I unravelled. Swallowed back up into my job and responsibilities, I didn't change anything. My anxiety got worse and worse, until that day in the car when I turned the steering wheel, and my car went careering off the motorway.

In the memory that my subconscious showed of my nan's bedroom, I smelt my nan's familiar smell, saw all of her things, felt the cold fur of her beautiful coats and the smooth surface of her immaculately made bed. Everything in her room was just so. Everything had its own place, but there were multiples of everything, drawers full of scarves, wardrobes full of suits, boxes full of jewelry, and shelves full of ornaments.

I realised as I revisited this safe and sacred place that these things held meaning for me. "Things" represented status, financial security, and sophistication. And safety. In believing in the security and status of these things, I had created that reality unconsciously in my home. My house was full of STUFF. I had held onto everything! I even realised I had SHIPPED boxes of crap from the UK when we moved such as teddies, ornaments, and photo frames. And through this nostalgic, subconscious tour, I had the awakening, first that my hoarding was completely unhealthy and once again, another pattern born out of scarcity over abundance, and second, that I'd been fearing the RISK of change, worrying that I would LOSE my husband for this radical change I wanted to see in my life and not see this massive opportunity to make things BETTER for everyone!

After this session, I began throwing and giving away all this mindless crap I had held onto for years. This was a major step on my journey forwards to freedom and the beginning of my external reality starting to match who I was on the inside.

Rebirth into an **Abundant Identity** requires death of all parts of your **Poverty Identity**. Trauma healing will enable you to identify the empowering beliefs that will allow you to live consciously in alignment with your Soul's Goal instead of surviving the illusions created from your limiting beliefs, which will only ever bring you the opposite of what you want and the reality you are trying to avoid.

And in releasing the grasp your **Survival Mind** has on your present moment, you can access the intuition that can show you the way to manifest your UNLEASHED vision easily. The universe is ALWAYS dropping signs and "breadcrumbs," but you miss them because your eyes are so fixed on the strategies, plans and lists you think are going to help you. You exist in your truth in your heart, so you have to be able to listen to your heart and how you feel about certain actions.

I began to let my emotions guide what I did in a positive way. This is why I am finally able to write this book! The conditioning I imposed on myself that the book needed to be a certain structure or a plot no longer binds me to procrastination, and I am able to open up my heart and let the words flow with ease. I actually couldn't care less if you think this book is good or not.

I overcame my fear of judgement to lead a mission and share a message I believe is important. I believe the Universe is supporting me because my intention is now to keep healing and living in the frequency that will heal the planet, instead of surviving in the victim consciousness that is creating the problems the world has. I am committed to taking action on the things that are important, instead of living by my excuses. I am guided by the intention to serve others who might be stuck like I was instead of playing small to stay safe.

The energy behind this intention is my purpose. And now this energy flows like the current of a river rather than it being blocked like it was behind a dam of emotions that were blocking my success with such deep energetic conflict. I am the source of my abundance, and I get to feel that abundance every day I continue to actualise my Soul Goal. So, my abundance comes from what I give, not what I gain.

"Wealth." "Rich." "Abundance."

When you say these words, it would seem they are things you gain from external sources, right? "Wealth" from the money you earn, the lotto you win or the inheritance your family hands you down. "Rich" with possessions, assets and a big number in your bank account. An "Abundance" of good luck showering down, money, love, and things that make you happy.

The truth, I realised, is that "wealth," being "rich" and "abundance" are none of those things. They are *feelings* you create yourself from the experience of how you show up in your life and GIVE yourself to whatever situation you are in. I've realised you can even feel abundant and grateful in the middle of the most challenging situations if you believe there is the opportunity for meaning, alignment and growth in them. How you move through any situation will always be guided by your perspective of it.

Changing my perspective in this way was like when the tide pulls a wave away from the shore and leaves a glistening crystal light shimmering on the sand. The light was HOPE of the difference I could now make with the illusion of scarcity pulled away by the gravity of the earth.

I reached out to Iracambi, the organisation I had volunteered with in Brazil, and I told them that I wanted to become an official sponsor of their cause, and we began to plan how this book could support them.

The thing I have realised while coaching so many people across the years is that every single one of us has been through things that have damaged us. We've all fallen in some way and gotten back up wearier and more cautious. Maybe we have fallen multiple times, and each time got back up even more weary than the time before. We then shrink our world to be able to live with all our fear, or we shrink our personality to fit within the confines of our limits. What about living BIG? What about limitless EXPANSION? In the introduction of this book, I told you that I would help you begin to live again with as much wonder as your 5-year self did. No more limits. No more seeing the risks before the adventure. Remember, your 5-year-old self had no concept of time, and everything was an adventure waiting for you to take it.

No more beating yourself up for what you don't achieve. No more shame. No more feeling unworthy, not good enough, unliked, or a burden on those around you. No more feeling sad, angry, or hopeless. *This is your TRAUMA, not your truth.* It is time to swap the story that impacted your sense of safety, worth, empowerment, lovability, and the feeling of being whole and good enough as you are for deep appreciation for yourself, a world that is beautiful and the trust that the world is a safe and magical place.

When I was in the UK in 2022, writing the final edit of this book and visiting my parents after a 4-year separation during Covid, I watched my dad cry multiple times. Cry at the sad songs. Cry at the post on Facebook he saw my niece write about her mum who we lost to cancer. Cry by whatever memories were being triggered as he was remembering were being lived right there in that moment again.

We busy ourselves in life so we don't feel, but when you can journey through the limiting beliefs created from your past experiences, the fire of your vision will burn stronger than the fears that have held you back and the sadness you hold from your past. Your pain will turn to gratitude and purpose.

Your purpose doesn't need to be grand or even about impacting anybody else apart from yourself, it just needs to drive you and make you feel, when you are moving towards the horizon of it, like your soul is doing a happy dance. You'll be able to listen to the sad song and hear it in a completely different way. I always used to feel sad listening to "Somewhere Over the Rainbow" because it was another song that reminded me of my nan. I think we even played it at her funeral. But now I hear it differently and smile. What a beautiful proposition that such a world could live at the other side of a rainbow.

As we change and heal our internal condition, our circumstances start changing around us and "luck" starts to come easily because the inside of us changes first. Our heart heals, and we can feel and let go of all the painful memories of the past and find flow.

We dissolve our trauma, literally by changing the lens through which we see our past. I created a Method I call **The Lens Process** to help people do this. We use it in the second part of the *Quantum Leap Method* to work with the mind and body to fully let go of pain, bitterness and regret, shift out of victim consciousness, get out of survival mode into love and forgiveness and to identify empowering belief systems that support neuroplasticity.

Before healing my trauma, I hit obstacle after obstacle and felt constantly lost, frustrated and confused about my purpose in life. I felt like I was stalled on a runway, waiting to take off, and helping no one, including me.

You don't have to change the world. If you can just change one person, it counts. And that person can be you. If you transform yourself, you'll transform the world anyway. Iracambi share a legend about a hummingbird that works to put out the flames in the forest while all the other animals stand stunned by their fear. Even though she can only carry tiny drops of water in her beak and she has to fly back and forth she proclaims to the animals watching her work, "I am doing my part."

As you read this book, you will see blank pages. They are blank for you to write your message of hope. Maybe you will pass this book onto another, or somebody passed this book on to you and so you have found a page with their message. Maybe we can create a global chain of giving and impact other as people find new ways of living on purpose.

My Soul Goal is to create a movement of people becoming the change the world needs to see and going on to help others, so there is a ripple effect. This book is the start.

PRACTICAL INTEGRATION

JOURNALING

Connect with the idea that all the way through your life you have been creating your internal programming—your internal operating system—your Blueprint from the experiences that you have had. Write down all the things you believe about yourself and the world and then ask yourself if they are really true or not.

For example, at school, we take on the belief that we need to have a good education and a good job to live a safe and productive life. Is this really true? Some of the most epic millionaires I know failed to finish school and made millions self-employed in their own business.

Many things we have been conditioned to believe come from a system that was set up to protect us in life. I began to question many things and wonder whether they were "truths" for me. Or were they just beliefs that worked for someone else at some point in history. I'm giving you full permission right now to do the same thing. Question your beliefs, especially if your life has started to feel uncomfortable and things don't seem to "fit" anymore. Maybe you are starting to feel that your potentiality is untapped and are wondering why you don't feel fulfilled or accomplished. You are asking the same questions I did... Who am I? Why was I put on this earth? What is the value I was born to deliver and the impact I was meant to make? Why am I doing the things that no longer feel like they are serving me in my life?

MANIFESTATION AND THE MIRACLE FREQUENCY

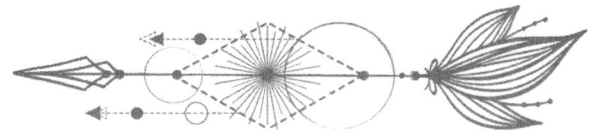

HOW TO CHANGE YOUR REALITY IN AN INSTANT

"I dream my paintings, then paint my dream."
VINCENT VAN GOUGH

The first section of this book talked about my past. Now I am going to start to share how I created my future.

That day in 2017 in the food bank was as low as I could go. My heart was broken. My pride was raw. My candle of hope was nearly burned away completely. Thankfully, my tiny shift in focus that came from a powerful intention from the core of me said, "I don't know how, but everything is going to change," created the oxygen that brought my candle back from dark to light. It rekindled my hope and the opportunity to work on myself, which by this point was the only thing I hadn't tried yet! Finally, after all the business strategies, budgeting plans, jobs, business opportunities, other's advice, etc., my focus turned inwards to my own thoughts, feelings, words, and ultimately, my heart and Soul Goal.

I even told my Muay Thai coach that I was going to take time out of fighting to train my mind instead of my body because it was crystal clear that my thoughts were not serving me, and it was affecting how I was showing up in the ring. I felt like I couldn't live in my own mind anymore feeling how I felt, and it wasn't healthy to keep avoiding feeling at all by living in the gym. It suddenly became clear that my mind was the wall between me and the actions that would change my life.

And that's the thing, right? Everybody in this world today is feeling. Feeling stressed, feeling heartbroken, feeling rejected, feeling unworthy, feeling anxious, feeling depressed. And yet everybody is focused on thinking their way out of their feelings or escaping them in unhealthy ways. How I committed to my Muay Thai gym (my husband joked I'd still train even if I had a broken leg) was really unhealthy and 100% a way to avoid both thinking and feeling. It had replaced my addiction to writing myself off with drink. And to be honest, in between fight camps, I would still write myself off with drink because I didn't have training as an incentive not to.

So, how do you change things and awaken your Miracle Frequency so that everything in your life changes without you having to work so hard for it? How do you focus on plenty if there is currently lack in your life? How do you take your focus away from the problem when the problem penetrates every area of your life? How do you remove the label you have placed over your situation for such a long time? How do you change your perception of wealth and success? How do you allow yourself to feel when the pain hurts?

I've already given you half the answer to that. It starts with intention, and it comes full circle with action. And sometimes action is doing nothing at all! If you are stuck right now, you can ask yourself a powerful question, are you doing **everything** you can to create your success? I know if you are truly honest with yourself you will say no, because like me, you have blocks. You acknowledge there is potential for shifts in your mindset. I'm going to suggest it goes deeper than that. And it's likely that the journey **inward** is one you have yet to take fully. You may have begun to take it, but you have *thought* your way through the steps, instead of feeling your way into your soul.

Ultimately, nothing changed in my life until I took my healing to a mind, body and spirit level. And until I acknowledged the potential that my financial hardship was not due to my circumstance at all. It was a consequence of my internal condition and the state it was in. Those words from my Coach Lesley whose message, "*Your External Abundance Reflects Your Internal Abundance*" was a wakeup call.

When I began to heal the wounds from my past, remove the armour I had worn for so long and change the perception of my reality, my reality began to physically change. I can't explain it, but money started to appear from the most unexpected places and there began to always be just enough for us to get by.

In order to lift "getting by" to more "wealthy" experiences, I learned I simply had to "unleash" my vision even further, but coming full circle again from whatever limiting beliefs and stories were coming up, so my vision expanded, my feelings changed, and I created and attracted differently. That is the difference between hustling for your success and inspired attraction and magnetic attraction; the Universe starts to support you to achieve your goals. You awaken your Miracle Frequency.

For me, the blocks I had in my business began to disappear, new ideas for its growth began to flood in like somebody had taken the floodgates away. Don't let anyone ever tell you that you aren't the most powerful tool in your business. Or the most powerful creator in your life. Within you are all the answers, all the ability to succeed, and all of your purpose for walking upon this earth at all. To connect with all of it, you must set the intention to invest in yourself first, every day. And you must give up thinking and learn to create high vibrational energy (even in the dark times) in order to master energetic coherence and access the infinite possibilities of the Quantum Field.

Before we start on these life-changing principles, you must know that without deep inner work, the Law of Attraction creates separateness that will sabotage your goal to manifest with ease. *This is because desire comes from a place of attachment to the outcome.* Manifestation comes from unwavering belief, desire that is intense and TRUST. For our dreams to manifest, we must be in energetic coherence. The likelihood is that if you have tried to manifest previously using visualisations and affirmations and it hasn't worked... this is why.

Coherence is the state when the Mind and Heart are in energetic alignment and balance. In practice, this is like your mind slowing down and carrying the same energy as what the heart feels. If you imagine yourself in your business right now, you may have stress over money, you may be wondering how you will pick up your next client, you may be confused about your business strategy, which is all an energy of scarcity. In your heart you might be desiring MORE. You want MORE income, more impact and maybe even more influence; you are ready to be known for what you do and unleash your Inner Millionaire!

For effective Manifestation of everything you want, what your mind thinks must be in alignment with what your heart feels. And maybe in your heart you really feel FEAR. You doubt yourself. You've been trying to think abundant thoughts, doing the affirmations, etc. "Feeling" is the most important factor in Manifestation. When you feel abundant, truly abundant in every essence of you, which means you feel as if you already have what you want, you will attract abundance. You might say, "I do feel abundant," but I'd proffer that your unconscious energy is potentially sabotaging your ability to manifest your dream life if you don't already have everything you want.

There are other factors in that as well, in that there is always a greater plan held by the Universe for you. What you really have to do is be absolutely clear about what you love and learn to trust that the Universe will provide that to you as long as you give in exchange. When you truly feel abundant, you show up differently in your life to when you are feeling scarcity. And this is the silent contract you have with the Universe. Give freely through your energy, feel elevated emotions, and live in a state of Coherence where your thoughts and feelings are aligned. Having all these pieces of the puzzle together is how you crack your Abundance Code, and it is what is creating fast results like my client's experience, regularly.

To recap:

- Desire alone is not enough to create a state of coherence;
- Without coherence, you will struggle to manifest OR find that the strategies you apply in your business don't work

easily either;

- Without belief and trust you dissipate the energy of what we call "the quantum feedback loop" that is created by your intention. We will dig into this in more detail, but effectively, to manifest easily, you return the energy of your intention back to you through your focus on the feelings you want, as if you have what you want already. This keeps the feedback loop strong. If you seek external validation that what you want is coming, instead of focusing on feeling the elevated emotion as if you already have it, that says that what you want is not already here, so the energy of your intention dissipates away, the feedback loop weakens, and you may not see the manifestation of your desire at all.

What strengthens the feedback loop and manifestation of your desires:

1. Hacking your limiting emotions, so you can release the fears, self-esteem blocks and disempowering beliefs that take your focus away from elevated feelings and get you focusing on the thoughts in your survival mind

2. Knowing your truth, taking radical responsibility for your Soul Goal and being truly in alignment with your purpose

3. Surrendering to your truth and having trust

4. Trusting yourself. This includes trusting yourself to look inwards for the answers to your problems in your business and trusting when it is time to "hire out." For example, I believe the most powerful messaging and marketing will come from within yourself but hiring some brand support or team to take on tasks is powerful.

5. Learning how to connect to divine assistance by accessing your Ultramind. If you are here on purpose/for service, you will always be guided by a higher power.

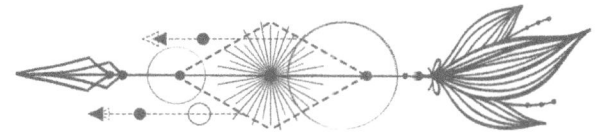

HACK YOUR LIMITING EMOTIONS

*"Feel blessed every single day, even if you don't
think you are."*
CLARE WILLIAMSON

I t's not easy to rebirth into an Abundance Identity when you have been living in one of scarcity for a long time. In many personal development books, and out of the mouths of many mentors, regularly come the words, "I believe, I think, you should, you shouldn't, etc." Everybody is always advising you from their perspective, their lens and their experience, and I really want to try to not do that. I made a pact with myself when I started coaching that I would never advise and that I would always learn to keep asking better quality questions to help people find the answers that they are seeking for themselves.

Obviously the more I have learned about growing a business, the more I have become a hybrid of a Mentor and a Coach, but I still try to coach wherever possible! Being coached isn't often the easy way. We want the Mentor to tell us how to do it, and this can be great... but it can also sabotage the learning path to the answer you are seeking. With the Mentor, you get the fast result, but you get it without the emotional intelligence, learned wisdom and experience that will mean you can handle it and you may find yourself misaligned.

In spite of this, we'll choose the Mentor because the writing isn't on the wall for us and that feels uncomfortable. We are not willing to sit out the discomfort to learn the lesson we need. We need to move forward NOW.

DISCOMFORT.

It feels like shit, but I promise you, it's the fastest route towards an Identity of Limitless Abundance that will change your life. And it is the power of Transformational Coaching to have an ally to help you broaden your perspective and thus your paradigm and help the learning you need for expansion to come strong and fast. And support you, so you can handle it!

When I came out of university and got my corporate job, I climbed up the ranks quite quickly and achieved a lot in a short time. My passion for the environment and tenacious way of being helped me to transform the environmental footprint of the portfolio of shopping centres I was supporting. With one in particular, I took their recycling rate up from about 15% to 60%, renovated the food court with these amazing bins and signs and got all the retailers on board with our movement and excited about saving the planet. I even won a prestigious award for my achievements!

I couldn't handle the fast growth though. When we went to the awards night, I got so drunk that I remember at one point I couldn't get off the toilet seat and my partner (now husband) had to find me. I was legless. I remember looking at the girls I had been up against and feeling like they were more deserving of the award than I was, and I felt ashamed to even be there.

I couldn't figure out how the hell I'd won. And there I was, the winner, this hot-shot young facilities manager having to be held up to stand and having to leave the event early. In front of all my bosses, the big wigs in the company, I was a wreck. Now I know I was battling my self-worth demons. I didn't feel good enough, and I certainly didn't feel like I deserved it. I was carrying this subconscious feeling of shame for being the girl who went to South America and got raped.

I believe that as time moves on from trauma, how you think about what traumatised you traumatises you even further. I had gone over that night in my mind, 1,000 times, at least and taken meaning from the fact that out of all of the girls that had gone out that night in Chile, I was the one who had ended up in the situation I did. That resonated with what my dad used to say about me being a "slut" in my clothes. Wearing short skirts only to attract the attention of boys. It resonated with how my mum made me feel about getting stuff wrong as a child and making bad decisions. I hated myself, and in the years that followed my experience in Chile, I went on a mission to cause my own self-destruction.

When I'd left for the trip to South America, I'd felt like I had the world in my hands. I was so authentically me. I felt the call of freedom, and I felt the adventure of the trip through every cell of my being. Travel was the one thing I had always wanted to do. Travel, write and save the rainforests. They were my constants. And as I lived through that incredible experience, I did both, and I felt alive. More alive and free than I had ever been before. The trip I took through Peru, Ecuador and Bolivia over Christmas time and the summer break was close to perfect. The dream trip. I was high on life and flying high. I didn't need to sort out my re-accommodation in Chile in advance because honestly, I felt like I could go anywhere the wind was taking me. I was free!

But in my mind, after that night, after the experience I'd had, freedom became something to fear and that fear would go on to affect how I showed up in every area of my life. I got into this pattern of control and self-sabotage if I got too close to success because it felt dangerous. It felt dangerous because I didn't trust myself, and I punished myself consistently for that flaw. I didn't trust that freedom wouldn't end up screwing me over again. So, I screwed up jobs. I would get super fit in the gym and then get drunk to spoil it. I would always find a way to land myself back up somewhere that felt like that familiar feeling of safety even though safety felt rubbish.

If you're not experiencing elevated emotions in connection with your intentions that keep your mind focused on abundance, you won't create the strong intentional current—the quantum feedback loop— that will help you manifest that success in your life.

You will stay in the lack, the failure, and the loneliness. Like a record going round and round, replaying the emotions of the past—*how it made you feel then*—rather than feeling the intense pleasure of the present, despite the circumstances you find yourself in.

In contrast, when you elevate emotion and start living into every moment of life, something magical happens. Life starts happening for you. This is the magic of awakening your Miracle Frequency!

Struggle doesn't necessarily go away, and there will always be challenges, but how you view them and respond to them will determine how you become a magnet to synchronicity and miracles.

Are you ready now to UNLEASH your highest potential?

$$\boxed{\text{PRACTICAL INTEGRATION}}$$

1. THE JOY GPS

This is a powerful tool that we use in the *Quantum Leap Method* to help you discover the things that set your soul on fire and especially the things that make you feel eternally happy when you are doing them. Basically, you get a little notepad that is small enough to carry around with you, and when you feel really good or happy in a moment, you journal what the moment was. Think of it like the GPS in a car. The GPS screams at you when you go in the wrong direction, "Recalculating! Turn around!" The Joy GPS is screaming at you the opposite. It's your heart screaming at you, "You are going the right way! Keep doing more of that!" We don't listen to our heart when we are scared by everything we fear. Now is when you are going to start. You can even start the journal every day with three things that you are grateful for.

2. GIVE UP SAYING "I CAN'T AFFORD IT" FOR ONE WEEK.

I did this for an entire year and watched my life completely change. When I wanted to say "I can't afford it," I said "This isn't a priority" instead. The transformation was unbelievable. Do this and you'll bring into consciousness how your unconscious energy is sabotaging the manifestation of what you want.

3. START TO MAKE DECISIONS LIKE YOU ALREADY HAVE EVERYTHING YOU WANT IN YOUR LIFE.

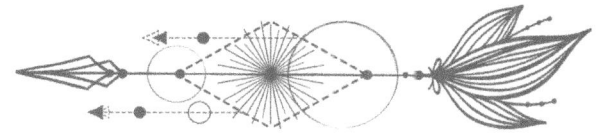

"YOU CAN HAVE IT ALL AND IT CAN BE EASY"

"Start saying yes to your yes."
DEREK RYDALL

M y soul has pulled me numerous times in directions I decided not to take because of my fears. For example, when I came out of university and put my resume up on some job finder site, I got offered the opportunity to work in Sorrento as a translator. This was a place on my bucket list because it had been somewhere my nan had loved so much and I wanted to see why. But ultimately, I turned the job down because I feared it wouldn't give me the security and safety I was seeking.

Right now, I am sitting writing the final draft of this book from 11,000 miles up in the air on a flight to Mexico, ready to take my amazing clients through a 4-day Transformational Retreat that I know they will remember for the rest of their lives.

I say yes to my yes ALWAYS, especially when I'm scared!! I remembered the day my Coach challenged me to do something that scared me and that was the birth of the Retreat idea. I kept saying yes along every part of the retreat creation, even when it felt illogical (like investing $10K on a retreat I hadn't sold yet).

I'm listening to a couple on the plane right now, sharing their holiday plans, and I'm thinking... "Isn't it funny the conditioning "life" has created that makes holidays a thing at all?" Now I know that ultimately, when we slow down, are mindful, stay in the moment, control our thoughts, look after our self-care, connect with what we love and our dreams every day and adopt an attitude of gratitude that holidays lose their meaning. It's just that life doesn't condition us to make these daily habits a priority. And as a Coach, I see people defend their excuses for living a life that goes against all those daily habits like there is an award for it because of their scarcity fears. I just want to reach out and embrace them and say, "It's okay. I was you. I was where you are. I couldn't see the problem either. I can help you, if you let me."

So, a few let me in when I had just started my journey of coaching. Now, many want my support because they see the results I have created for myself and others, but they struggle to take the leap of faith that is required to pay for my programmes or they invest cheaply in an online programme where they aren't directly supported and then they don't do the work.

I used to find it really frustrating, but then I realised it came back again to INTENTION. With the right intention, you will part with the investment in a different energy to the person who is stuck in a victim consciousness and behind their blocks because of their fear of scarcity and their allegiance to their busyness. For a long time, I would try to convince people to work with me from the perspective of my own scarcity mindset and offer them my support for free ("but I need to help you now!") and those who would take my support would literally take it and do nothing, while those who had invested money would completely transform their life. It took me a long time to understand that those who will invest in help are serious about their own growth and will decide with energy and intention that will transform their life. They transform themselves and their mindset in ways that make them unrecognisable to the person they were before.

In 2019, I took part in a reality show. I did it because I needed the prize they were offering with every cell of my being. Despite the mindset work I had done, I wasn't seeing success, so I felt like I needed more coaching only I didn't believe I could afford to pay for it.

The reality show was called *Play to Win*, and it was like the Apprentice, but for Network Marketers. You went on, took sales challenges and faced tough business interviews only we didn't know any of this or really what they were looking for from us until we were filming the first day of the show. It was the first time the show had ever been done, and we'd had no information in the lead up. But that was the challenge! To show up unfiltered, persuasive, and playing to win, despite everything else. We were "playing to win" a job or a coaching prize from the Higdon Group, a Fortune 500 company in the States that was growing like wildfire.

I wanted to win the coaching to grow all areas of my business, my life coaching and network marketing. At the foundation of that, I wanted help to build a brand that brought the two things together. I wasn't sure of my "Superpower," the driving force of a brand and the impact I wanted to create. In the reality show, I did identify it, but I also identified the "kryptonite" that had always and would always threaten it—that persisting fear and my survival mind.

"IT IS NOT FEAR'S TURN NOW, IT'S MY TURN."

These were the words I'd said in my interview at the *Play to Win* reality show. We had two interviews on the first day of competition. The first was with the film crew to get a background of "our story," and the second was with the judges about why they should pick us for the prize.

I had a very contradictory experience across the two interviews. In the first, I was recounting my previous two years' journey of mindset work, strength and vision. Then, in the interview with the judges, all that mindset, strength, and vision disappeared. I completely lost my voice, questioned everything I believed I had learned about myself and was affected by the judge's questions. The hold my survival mind had over my need to be able to edit, elaborate and filter so I was good enough caused me to "fold" under the pressure of the cameras, the lights and the judges. I lost my voice. I was required to speak straight from my heart, and I couldn't. Fear muted me. All the lights went on in my mind, and I saw it as clear as day. I was stuck in my story, and it caused me to lose the reality show in the end. I got close though! I made the finals, but leaving ultimately without the prize, left me in a kind of a No Man's Land.

It was like I'd chucked my last dollar at the roulette table and lost it. At first, I had no idea what to do next. I sat on the plane flying home sitting in the seat I had yet to pay for because

I'd had to put half my flight tickets on a credit card, and just stared into space.

Everything felt surreal. I even thought about this book and whether I should keep writing it. I thought about my coaching and whether I should bother to keep trying to build it. I thought about those first few weeks in my network marketing business and all the hope I had in my heart for a better future and remembered sitting in a zoom chat with Lesley when she'd asked me to talk about what I wanted for my life. I remembered how hard it was to see anything at all.

And then suddenly, out of nowhere, a light bulb went on in my mind. Why I went into that show and put everything on the line squeezed me around my throat so hard that I couldn't breathe until I picked up a pad, a pen and began to write! I wrote down three massive right-now goals, the three things I wanted that being on the show had really helped me get clear on. Then, I thought honestly about the vehicles I needed to achieve those goals, and the person I had to become to take the steering wheel and drive.

As I was doing that, the vision of my life started coming together. Events, travelling, speaking with my business. A beautiful, but modest house on the beach with white walls and a bunch of kids around an island in a big kitchen eating breakfast to the sounds of the waves. All of us travelling together all over the world for education, for pleasure, and to give to people less fortunate than ourselves. Me working with my beloved rainforest project, Iracambi, a dream lost to the scarcity in my life.

As I drew this vision out onto my notepad, the tears started to flow. I could see how, as my future self, I was making decisions from a place of abundance. In my vision, my "riches" were an abundant choice of the wealth of time, freedom, generosity, love, and fulfilment to work achieving my mission in life to make a difference, my Soul Goal.

HOW HAD THIS SOUL GOAL GOTTEN SO LOST?

When I was a child, giving, adventures, and "being on a mission" defined me. These activities were how I spent most of my time. You've heard me talk about WWF and the animals, I also spent all my time outside adventuring and often got hooked on missions to save the planet. The remainder of my time was spent hanging out in my room, listening to music, writing, reading, and daydreaming. There was so much time back then. And so much time is spent just passing time. We don't do so much of that as adults. There is always a to-do list, a responsibility, something worrying us, or something pulling us from just stopping to be.

I realised coming home from that experience in the reality show that a lot of people are running from themselves, exactly like I was. Running from feeling what it really is that is holding them back because it hurts like hell. In the show, there was nowhere to run. And because of that, I connected with all the pain I had spent 14 years running away from. I stood in it knee deep, and I cried instead of showing up and winning that competition. I cried instead of using my voice to pitch the ideas that would make the judges pick me as winner. I felt so frustrated with myself!

But on the plane home, I remembered something that the previous two years had taught me. That when we feel struggle like that, we are right on the edge of a breakthrough. There is just something we have to learn—clarity of our purpose, belief, skills, strategy—one or all of them before the light shines through.

It became really clear to me that I needed to figure out what the hell I wanted and why I wanted it. Not the hazy outline. The specific details. And as I did, I was able to see it and feel it like I was already doing it, already experiencing the results, filled with the energy and feeling of all the fulfilment and success.

I suddenly believed I was BORN to coach. It was like a glove that was a perfect fit, like wearing Cinderella's glass slipper, like putting on an outfit and owning it because you feel amazing and want everyone to see. Coaching was the only thing I did well the whole time on the reality show. When people struggled or I saw that they were holding themselves back, I stepped in. I shone. I knew what to do, what to say, how to help them. On the plane that day I wrote out a 125 Day Action Plan that would take me up to the Higdon Group's next event, where I set the intention that I would speak on their stage with my message and mission concisely and powerfully communicated.

However, when I got home, everything changed. I was met with my own resistance. I felt like I was pulling my feet through deep mud when it came time to take the actions I had identified in my 125 Day Plan. Writing this book ground to a halt because I didn't want to feel everything that the idea of telling my story to the world made me feel.

The feeling of shame was coming up a lot, and I know now it was at the root of the resistance, but I didn't then. I just experienced the "symptoms." Sharing on social media like I'd planned to felt hard. I'd promised myself I'd start doing regular live videos, but I didn't feel like showing my true self, with my unfiltered thoughts and less than perfect reality, to a world I was trying to convince that I was something I suddenly felt I wasn't again.

Suddenly, the vision of my superstar coaching future also became a joke in my mind, and I questioned who I was trying to kid thinking I could have any of it. I started fearing the reality show airing. I didn't feel like the girl they would see in the show, but I also didn't feel like the girl who had "existed" for 14 years before the show, and I didn't know who I had to become to feel at home in my heart.

FREE OF SHAME. Free from the dirtiness of the rape and my childhood, free from the guilt I felt about not being able to help my mum in her illness and for being a burden to her struggles and the struggles of my dad, and free from the shame of never ever being good enough. In not becoming free of these feelings, I knew I was fighting for a life that was out of alignment with my true Soul Goal, but right then and there, I still couldn't figure out what was missing that would unleash my untapped potentiality and the soul purpose that I could now feel fighting to come out.

Thankfully, in a moment of inspiration while I was still in the airport clearing customs, etc., off the plane from Fort Myers, Florida on May 31st, I decided to offer a free month of coaching that I would invite every woman and her mate to join, starting June 1st. I promised "30 days of powerful coaching to break through the limits of yourself by discovering yourself in all your true, authentic power and purpose."

I had no choice, but to work really hard on this. I was up late every night creating the content for the next day because it pushed me to go live on Facebook, and I was also taking the steps in the content myself. My intention was to bring the whole world along with me on this journey of enlightenment. All those people fighting themselves, stuck in their story. Who wouldn't grab the chance to have free coaching?

Fortunately, everybody did grab the free coaching!! Unfortunately, nobody wanted to pay for more after the free coaching finished. And this was the wakeup call I needed to snap me out of my resistance. I realised that, once again, I was doing something because I needed something. I needed the clients. And finally, the message came to land. My Scarcity Identity had ruled the show, again. Like was attracting like. How could I judge these people when I was exactly the same?! Was I paying for coaching? The fight I'd had with myself to buy those flight tickets to Florida had been excruciating. My focus in offering coaching was on making money because I needed it. This same need meant that when I lost the *Play to Win* competition, all I had seen and felt was the scarcity instead of the many blessings that came out of the experience.

Finally, it was becoming clear—my need was not going to get me anywhere in life. It hadn't gotten any of the contestants in the *Play to Win* show anywhere either. The judges had been looking for value, what we could GIVE. Ray Higdon had asked this epic question... "How can you show up in a way that means you get picked first?" I was so focused on gaining clients at the end of that free coaching, I had forgotten its original intention, to give help and value. I felt frustrated and bitter by the fact people had taken advantage of free coaching and not bought anything instead of focusing on creating an experience that would guarantee they would want to continue working with me! It was time for this message to land and it finally did.

At some point, a small percentage of us reach a point where fear, playing small and our victim consciousness is no longer serving us and the Awakening begins.

For me, the shift that enabled me to see the perspective I did when nobody bought my coaching offer was understanding everything I had to lose by continuing to give into my fear. I had to experience my fear of being vulnerable and in doing so, I connected with my Soul Goal, my purpose. Before Florida and the *Play to Win* Show, I had used this affirmation that Lesley helped me create to ease my anxiety—*I am embodying the absence of trust and feeling myself fly*—but I suddenly saw how I needed to be able to experience the fall.

Remember, a new experience creates a new emotion and for me, because I'd done something that had pushed me out of my comfort zone enough to give me a totally new experience, I'd not only got to see my own capability, but I'd also gotten to feel how good it felt to actually help people and make a difference! This set alight a fire in my soul so fierce that my perspective on everything started to change.

Instead of feeling the failure of the launch, I felt the fire of being better and continuing to find my voice!

The safe bubble of a world that I had existed in for 14 whole years had finally become toxic. I found the strength to end the pattern of making decisions from inside that bubble, thinking from inside that bubble and taking action from inside that bubble, and I found the strength to do it AUTHENTICALLY. To make the impact I was born to make just by being myself. No filters. No more overthinking and editing my actions through the safety filter of my mind. Just open, raw, and honest, speaking my truth, even if my voice shook.

After the failed launch, I started showing up on video online nearly every day and began to trust in what I had always been told. I could run my business off the simple DMO (daily method of operation) of a live video that added value, content that connected with people and conversations that were to the point and purposeful with people directly every day. In terms of workload, this was EASY compared to what I had been doing but letting go of the conditioning that my success required more was hard.

I also had to go through the discomfort of feeling exposed doing the live videos and standing for what I believe, rather than what I thought others wanted to hear. It required risking the fact that someone might call me out on what I believe. It required being vulnerable. And my mind continued to fight me to be quiet, but my determination was suddenly stronger.

I was suddenly able to push through the original low motivation I'd experienced hitting my own resistance. I used mantras to help me take action, like "I have no excuses" or if I found myself comparing myself to other coaches I would say, "My frustration is my trigger to give more, not give up!" This is the difference between "showing up" with the intention to prove everything is possible and "showing up" taking action to prove your limiting beliefs. While I did allow the excuses to not to show up get the better of me some days, on more days than not, I was starting to FLY. I was even pushing through the instinct to script my videos, which edited how I truly felt, in the trust that I had something important to say at the right moment. I came up with the mantra, Feel, Think, DO! And, I used it every day. And every day, my DMO became a little easier.

GROWTH.

Growth has been a priority in my life since network marketing opened me up to the opportunity to start plugging into personal development daily. In my first few weeks of coaching with Lesley, she said "80% of your work should be on you" and I laughed! How could that possibly be? How would I pay the bills if I wasted time on personal development instead of working to make money?

But it all makes sense now. The key to making money is YOU. It's what you give every day that will guide what you receive. The more you work from the inside out, the easier it will be to get everything you want. However, you have to recreate the experience I had in the reality show where I pushed my comfort zone enough to experience the vulnerability of what I feared, so that I had a revelation about what I am actually capable of.

You might be avoiding that at all costs right now because you aren't empowered to hack the emotions that are recycling the same negative thoughts you have every day, which is pulling your past into the present and sabotaging it and causing you to pull the past into the potential future, so that you are also sacrificing opportunity. And, you are running away from the truth of who you are.

As I showed up publicly, I started feeling more comfortable about letting my freak flag fly, so to speak. I realised it's okay to be different, it's okay to have quirks and dreams and ideas. It's even okay to be broken.

My previous lack of alignment with my true self and my Soul Goal had dulled my colour like a painting left out in the rain.

My life was a frustrating repeat of not feeling good enough and failing exactly because of that. It was affecting every area of my life, including my parenting. My life was being controlled by my fear and my limiting beliefs that I can't, that I'm not good enough, that I don't deserve, etc. But as I began to find alignment, my unhappiness lessened, and so did my anxiety.

I'd fought anxiety, up to this point, for 12 years. I haven't talked so much in this book about exactly how this debilitating condition affected me day to day. Perhaps that will be the subject of my next book, considering it is now the most prominent mental illness in the world, and it is so challenging to overcome. As I've already shared, I'd tried everything to relieve my anxiety and while I had some small progress, nothing had worked to fully take the anxiety away. I never woke up and had a day where I was feeling normal more than I was feeling the anxiety.

At one point, I forgot what feeling normal felt like. It is no coincidence to me that my big milestone in beginning to have those days when feeling normal did dominate came when I realised how out of alignment I was with my soul. Now I believe my fear was showing me where my life was not where my soul wanted me to be. Even my anxiety was a positive thing!

Play to Win was like finding the missing piece of a jigsaw puzzle that brings a full picture together. I realised two key things in the experience. That I didn't truly feel like I deserved to be what I was seeking to become and that I didn't have a clear picture of what that was. Fear was stopping me fully seeing the vision of a life that aligned to everything I truly was because of the fear that I wasn't good enough to have it. I had to become fierce about what I deserved and fully believe in the fact that I deserved it. Shamans call this arousing your inner fire. I share a lot of breathwork journeys on YouTube to help you do this.

THE ANTIDOTE TO FEAR IS CURIOSITY.

If we fear the unknown because it is something we have never had, we must create the vision that makes it known to us.

In the *Play to Win* competition, I got to see myself through the lens of other people, and it helped me create the vision of who I want to become. In your day-to-day life, you might not be getting that sort of perspective.

This is why working with a coach is so powerful. They will hold a mirror up to your life to show you a picture of how you are showing up, so you get to decide whether that is good enough for you. It can really be uncomfortable to see your limiting patterns, but as you have seen through my story and experience, if you push yourself out of your comfort zone enough, you will see opportunity.

A coach will ask the tough questions that nobody else is asking you, which you are avoiding by staying busy in the "motions of life." Through the lens of the judges and their feedback, I saw a girl who was scared to stand out, which makes sense now that you know my story, but I also saw how I couldn't create my future while still living in the past. I also saw my pain through their lens and got honest about the fact I hadn't spent much time healing my internal condition.

From the day the rape happened, I'd put all my energy into avoiding it, but in doing that, I'd put an armour on that which had detached me from reality and from the people I love or could grow to love. The first thing I did when I got home from Florida was tell my husband that I was sorry. As the tears flowed, I shared how I knew I had never given him 100% of myself, and I helped him to understand why. I released him from the belief it was something to do with him. It was one of the most open, vulnerable conversations we have ever had, and we both felt lighter for it. It also seemed to give him permission to talk about what he truly wanted in life, his dreams and his hopes.

My next step was to call my dad and open up to him about the rape. This wasn't about getting the burden off my chest or getting sympathy. It was about helping the people I loved the most to understand the person they had loved and lived with for the 14 years I'd been so broken. It had impacted them as well as me, and it gave them the relief of knowing that the stuff I had done, that they didn't understand, or had even blamed themselves for, was because of me, not them. I broke my parents' hearts when I left England for New Zealand. I know they believed in some part of them that it was because of them and the troubles we'd had. I wanted to absolve them of that guilt and as I shared the truth about the rape, my dad said everything made sense to him now. In using my voice to speak from my heart, I released some of his pain too.

So many of us are living on repeat of past experiences because we have become trapped within the limiting beliefs they have created. Trapped by fear. Trapped in the stories we tell ourselves about what happened to us, creating pain that we fight to push down instead of feel. It becomes a revolving circle of untruths guiding our perspective, decreasing our self-belief, and dictating the value we place on our abilities and worth.

I thought I hit rock bottom in the food bank that day, but upon reflection, my heart didn't break enough to truly open. It didn't in that experience of the reality show either, but something shifted, like no other shift I had previously experienced. That vision piece, the answer to the question I'd never truly answered about who I truly was and what I wanted finally came together, and I saw who I was away from my story and my excuses.

I was broken and open and raw enough to really see that my heart and my intuition had been lacking in the decisions I had made across the previous couple of years. I was still trapped in my head and letting my thoughts control my destiny, and it was time to give thinking a break. It wasn't getting me anywhere.

It was time to feel in my heart what I truly wanted to do and who I really was, what I really loved and how I could show up in my life with those beautiful qualities unique to me and add value to the lives of others. Doing this, I finally found my voice and my confidence, and I felt electric. I actually did speak on the Higdon's stage at that event later in the year!

My next step was to see who was going to catch my spark.

PRACTICAL INTEGRATION

JOURNALING

Are you running your life from a rule book that isn't yours?

Journal the answers to these questions:

1. Do you look forward to holidays because you feel like you need a break?
2. Do you feel like you are running on a hamster wheel and want to get off?
3. Do you feel like your wheels are spinning on the ground and you are not going forward despite your hard work?
4. Do you get sick a lot?
5. Do you feel like you aren't productive in your work or your life?
6. Do you feel frustrated, bitter and complain frequently?
7. Do you feel like you aren't creative or innovative and feel like your inspiration is blocked?
8. Do you find it hard to stop and take a moment to "contemplate the fluff in your navel" i.e., do absolutely nothing?

What do the answers to these journal questions tell you about your life?

For me, the uncomfortable awareness of my answers was where the journey of one seemingly crazy mother with two small children and not a penny to rub together really started. Things got really exciting from here on out! The discomfort gave me the push I needed to recover from a life I was spending just surviving.

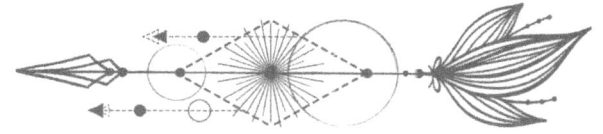

ACCESS YOUR ULTRA-MIND

"Three dreams take us away from our sacred dream: the dream of security, the dream of permanence, and the dream of love that is unconditional."
ALBERTO VILLOLDO

*T*o summarise, by the Law of Attraction, energy is the thing that will dictate the abundance you want to attract into your life. The energy of fear will manifest more of what you fear.

If you can remove fear from your life, you will manifest a beautiful, exhilarating and abundant life, easily.

The biggest thing we fear is scarcity, a scarcity of love and a scarcity of security, as Alberto Villodo defines, these come from the three dreams we all have that take us away from our **Sacred Dream** (what I like to call the "Soul Goal"), "the dream of security, the dream of permanence, and the dream of love that is unconditional."

In 2021, I actually realised I feared CREATIVITY because of a scarcity of belief in my own power, and this was significantly affecting me scaling my business and aligning my business to my Soul Goal. I was scared to try things in case I "got it wrong." I was struggling to take action on the ideas that I was brainstorming with my now, high-ticket coach, Niyc Pidgeon, who was pushing my comfort zones in all sorts of areas more than ever!

Yes. I invested in coaching.

I remember the day I signed up to Niyc's programme in November 2019. I was sick with the fear I had to override it to say yes! My husband had been made redundant from his job right before Christmas, and we had decided that for a few months, I would step in full time to my business, and he would "daddy day care" the children. He'd been given a little money for redundancy, and we put over half of it down as a deposit for Niyc, and we had no idea how we would make the second payment.

I remember asking Niyc the difference between someone who succeeds in her programme and someone who fails. She answered decisively. If I'm entering any doubt into the equation at this point, I'm already deciding I am not going to show up and do whatever it takes to succeed.

Shortly after I signed up with Niyc, Covid started. My husband had no choice but to stay off work as he physically couldn't apply for a new job, and I became the main breadwinner in the family. With a $3,000-dollar bill to pay every single month on top of our bills and expenses.

And I made that payment every single month without fail.

My experience is why, when I hear potential clients say, "I can't afford it"... I know they need it more than ever.

I'm living proof that you create a wave of energy just by how you think about entering in a situation That is the beginning of your quantum feedback loop. Then you feed the feedback loop by where you place your focus through the situation. If you allow your focus to continue to focus on everything that is lacking in your life and all your fear, you will 100% guarantee the scarcity of what you were fearing in the first place.

You have to break the pattern.

Your energy is creating your reality. The Universe is saying... "Your wish is my command!" Worrying is basically praying for everything you don't want.

When you even allow yourself to think, just for a moment, "I can't afford it," you are admitting DOUBT, and you are sealing your fate. You are also switching on your Survival Brain and switching OFF any possible access to your Ultramind, which needs you to believe with CERTAINTY that something is possible before it forms a powerful imprint on your brain stem that can redirect what you focus on and create a filter, so you only see opportunities to live out your Soul Goal.

Remember your *"Reticular Activating System"* (RAS)? The bundle of nerves at your brainstem that will seek out information from your environment and experiences to validate your beliefs and filter out anything unrelated to what you see as important?

This biological process not only works to your disadvantage when you are focusing on lack, it will work for your advantage when you shift your belief systems and your empowered belief systems will access the creativity that will make you succeed (and magnetic).

We can't access creativity in a survival state!

Just imagine an electrical wire for a moment, full of resistance... That's you with all your fear and negative energy. Imagine if you took all your fear and negative energy away, what would happen to the electricity? What would happen to you if you believed, just for a moment that you CAN, so that you switch on your Ultramind and start creating and attracting the reality you want.

I said, "I can't afford it" over and over again until I ran out of options and asked the question... "How can I make this happen?"

In 2019, I knew I needed to hear the truth that Niyc shared with me that day... But until then, I'd refused to invest in the type of coaching experience that would give me direct access to a good coach that asked great questions. And it showed. I was unclear, very confused and unsuccessful!

My fear of getting things wrong or saying the wrong thing were consistently triggering a subconscious train wreck of thought that always led to the same place and repeating negative patterns of inaction that weren't taking me forward to where I really wanted to be and just even attracting more scarcity to me.

A client said to me once, "Clare, what you do is literally the difference between a business making it or failing. I can't count how many times I have been on the edge of giving this all up. I've been praying for help so much, and then voilà, you appeared!"

Hearing things like this always lights my Soul fire. Especially when my clients are true Impact Makers with a powerful Soul Goal that will change the world.

If you are reading this right now and FEELING the deep calling to make a bigger impact on this world, but know you're being held back by your own fears, visibility wounds and not feeling good enough or feeling too small to make a difference, it's time to:

1. Stop fearing creativity, the unknown and your success

2. Activate your Miracle Frequency

3. Awaken your creative power and start alpha creating

#1 is just a decision—an intention—you can even make a pledge with me right now...

"I, [insert your name], hereby DECIDE to turn my whole life around.

There is a big difference between a choice and a decision. We all have the choice to change. If we are uncomfortable in our situation, we feel that choice penetrating our body. A burning wave of "should," "need," "often," and "Yeah, but…"

"Yeah, but I don't have time."

"Yeah, but I can't afford it."

"Yeah, but I don't know how."

A decision is different. A decision is final. It is acutely followed by action.

#2 Is your commitment to use the free resource I will give you in the final part of this book that will help you create space for creativity, synchronicity and miracles.

#3 Is the natural flow from steps 1 and 2. Successfully manifesting with the Law of Attraction is simply deciding, surrendering, trusting and taking aligned action.

I call this surfing the creative wave of chaos, where you stay in absolute trust of what is playing out for you in every moment, even if it's uncomfortable. In doing this, I have transitioned from a business that felt too small for my Soul Goal to a brand and a movement that is so big it terrifies me.

I have not always believed in the Law of Attraction. Somewhat ironically, my dad did. Back when he was trying to make his businesses work, he did some personal development. He went to a big Tony Robbins event and learned techniques he still uses to this day.

One thing I specifically remember him doing (maybe it was even after this event) was pasting the letters "PMA" every-where. I remember getting up for school one day and it was scrawled across the bathroom mirror in pink lipstick. Then we went down for breakfast, and it was pinned to the fridge. And then we went to leave the house, and it was on every door! PMA stood for Positive, Mental Attitude!

I now know that it was like an affirmation for him, a reminder that his mindset was important. Tony Robbins told him in that event that if he believed he could do it, he could do whatever he wanted, but it started with a positive mindset, which cre-ates a positive energy.

The energy of fear is low, dragging, and lifeless, so because like attracts like, we must raise our vibration to match the level of energy in the vision of the life we want, which requires pay-ing attention to how we feel about everything that happens around us in every moment.

Notice I say "happens around us." This is the start. To see that nothing is happening to you. You have total control over how you respond to everything!

After my lightbulb moment that I needed to invest more in myself after *Play to Win*, I started by investing in a digital course from Jim Rohn. In it, he said this epic quote... "Become a millionaire not for the million dollars, but for what it will make of you to achieve it."

Since then, I've heard other personal development greats like Sir Richard Branson, Mindvalley's Vishen Lakhiani, Tony Rob-bins, and many others say this same thing in many different ways.

And I believe that the arrival to this limitless abundance identity will save you from wasting another moment of your life and especially the next 40 years of your working life, or however much is left, living in struggle and dodging the realisation of your Soul Goal, your "BIG WHY."

It has taken me many years on from the "expected path of school, college and university" to question whether there was always an alternative path alongside the accepted path of "success" that I didn't see to take. One where you follow your own rules, not the rules that society created for the majority to live a life that is "safe." Generally, this means a life working hard in a job you don't really like that pays you just enough to fit your needs and pay for some nice wants on top. Where your fear keeps you in a comfortable box, where you never get to find out how powerful you can be.

And because of this conditioning and programming to stay within the boundaries of what is safe and known, we resist the Universe helping us to create what we truly want by reacting to our fears and trying to control how life plays out.

We do this rather than do what I have come to fondly describe as surfing the creative wave of chaos, where you stay in absolute trust of what is playing out for you in every moment, even if it's uncomfortable.

Your ability to handle discomfort decides which part of the brain you operate from: the Alpha Creative Brain and Ultramind or your limiting Survival Brain.

When I went on the *Play to Win* reality show, I was fully in my Survival Brain. I needed to win the support to grow my business because I wanted a better life, and nothing I was trying was working.

When I was in Florida, the day before the final filming, we had a chance to order "swag" from the Higdon Group branded merchandise that would be useful to our businesses. There was stuff I had been looking at for months prior to the event, and I had put off ordering it because of the big shipping cost to New Zealand. With that taken away, it made total sense to order the merchandise, especially considering the $5,000 cash prize that was up for grabs as a prize for the winner the next day.

All of a sudden, I found myself panicking. Adding up the cost of the merchandise I wanted came to a figure that I couldn't really justify, considering the investment to get to Florida and our financial situation at home, which was still challenging to say the least. But surely if I really believed in myself to win the prize, there should be no question other than to order the swag! I felt a tightening feeling around my throat, and my head started to spin. I was having a full-on panic attack. It was the fear that I would spend money I believed we didn't have enough of and in doing so contribute to us landing back where we had been a couple of years ago.

Drowning in scarcity, the place I feared the most. The scarcity that had represented my late childhood. The recurring pattern of my life. This fear catalysed a physical process—the beads of sweat that appeared on my forehead, the increase in my heart rate and breath rate, and the blood rushing from my gut.

I unconsciously did the right thing in the moment though, thanks to the tools I had learned across the previous couple of years. You see, we are empowered to act in a way that is positive only at this decoding stage of the physical process of emotion. We can choose to feel the emotion and question it, and in doing this, we process it, and it is not repressed. We can meet our needs and listen to the important messages of our inner voice.

After this point, the opportunity is gone, and the emotion becomes another warning signal that our brain needs to jump into the Survival Brain and protect us. The physical process becomes autonomous. When I challenged my feeling of fear in that moment of ordering the swag with a question—the question of whether I truly believed in myself to win the reality show prize—I reached rational reasoning and I took different action. All along, my inner voice had been telling me to go for it but the anxiety was my ego saying the opposite! It is that voice, the voice of our Survival Brain that wins more often than not because we listen to those more familiar thoughts in our head over the voice of our soul.

I finally opened my laptop and sent my "wish list" to the show crew. And then the anxiety was gone.

When we believe something with absolute conviction, it will manifest.

I didn't believe I was going to win that show, and I didn't. What is interesting though, is that as a runner up in the competition, I won a US$100 voucher to spend on swag, which was nearly two-thirds of the amount on my wish list! I believe my winnings just about matched where my belief was at the time.

The discomfort and the question of why this swag experience was so uncomfortable for me was still plaguing me when I got home from Florida and was part of my decision to invest in a second coach to help me, Derek Rydall, who is an Abundance

Coach. He taught me that when we look to things external to us from a place of need, there are BIG gaps we need to plug within us. My experiences in Florida proved I still had gaping holes to plug, and so I set the intention to start showing up because I wanted stuff that is aligned to my mission, values, abilities, passions, and soul goal, rather than out of need, PLUS I would learn how to trust that I am the source of my own abundance so that wholeness, joy, freedom, and purpose could weave through everything I do, every day of my life. And this state of wholeness would reflect as wholeness in my life.

What we focus on expands. We can focus and stand up for everything we are (abundance) or focus on and play to prove everything we are not (scarcity).

While our scars still mark us, we are in scarcity because the pull to rely on external sources to feel safe and secure (in our businesses, our relationships, and our bank balances) will always be greater than our trust in ourselves as the true source of our abundance because of our creative POWER. When the fire of my Soul Goal started to truly burn, it was the antidote to this need for safety and security and the armour I had been wearing to keep me safe and secure suddenly grew pins in it and became really uncomfortable.

My curiosity of what the life I really wanted could truly be like stoked the flames of that fire and when I felt that fire, I could do anything, in spite of any fear, and that energy, that vibration, was positively electric. It was like a drug! I just wanted to feel more of it! It could overcome the other bullshit thoughts keeping me safe and keeping me small.

Remember, you don't have to wait until you hit rock bottom to set the intention to change your life

When a crisis forces you to your knees, your head is in your hands, and the tears are flowing, you can either fall and stay down on the ground or set the intention to RISE. This was the "ah-ha" moment I had as I unpacked the boxes of food back at home from that food bank. It was just the smallest flash of insight, but it was enough to continue the change of flow in my energy so that both inspiration and opportunity showed up, and the journey to where I am today, healed and happy, started.

To connect with your soul goal, you must dig deep through many layers of armour. In the moment of crisis, or preferably before getting there, you have to set the intention to redis-cover yourself and love yourself in all your true, authentic and even flawed beauty.

You can do that right now if you want to.

It took me a long time to unlearn the shame of being me. For ages, when an impulse came to share something on social media related to my mission, I questioned whether someone would call me out for being wrong or attack my opinion.

What is crazy is that in 2021, someone did. I opened an email to read a million-dollar libel suit had been served to me from someone who had bought one of my digital courses because she felt like I had been talking about her on Instagram when I said you don't have to be a forever victim to PTSD.

I'm not going to lie. I shit myself opening that email, but I am grateful the discomfort confronted some of the limiting beliefs I was still carrying about myself and my voice. Ultimately my lawyer resolved the issue, which had no basis in truth, and I said thank you for the enlightenment I'd had because awareness is the key to growth.

That is why working with a coach is so powerful; they give you insight you don't have on yourself, and if you are not aware of something, how can you change it? How can you ask those powerful questions of yourself, those that will help you be in control of the decoding process of your emotions? I had a client hate me for telling her to breathe in the moment of her crisis. However, this is the moment you must change everything before the autonomic physical process of your nervous system begins and you react in a way that may not be aligned and seal your manifestation fate with your energy.

The lady who served the libel suit had been triggered by my post and reacted because she wasn't ready to grow and change her life. That was already evident to me because while she bought my course, she hadn't started it. Something had come up, and she no longer felt she could prioritise it, but ultimately, you can keep sitting and waiting for the right time or you can start by taking action today.

We keep growing until the day we die. All you have to do is begin.

I smile now when I think of my crazy old dad with his Post-it notes and his lipstick messages on the mirror. He began this journey too, only it's a two-way journey with the Universe, and the Universe has a plan. She is just waiting for the signals from you that you are ready and for your internal abundance to reflect the external abundance that she has in store for you. You will actually gain that abundance in material form in your life by giving of yourself to your situation of scarcity and struggle. Look at what you are not getting in your life and ask yourself honestly what you are not giving. What are you hiding away from because of fear? What situations do you need to give up instead of keep fighting? What can you do to be empowered instead of being defeated by whatever is challenging you?

When I began to shift my Scarcity Identity, I stopped waiting around until I could afford stuff, and I started asking the question, "How can I afford this?" "What can I do to make this happen?" Because the saying is right, opportunity waits for no man. If the Universe offers out her hand and you reject it, that opportunity is gone.

How many opportunities are you going to give away because you think you can't afford it? Can you afford not to change the direction of your life? It's your turn to feel what is at stake and commit to taking bold action. The Universe can only return it because of the Laws of Attraction. There is confidence in alignment and purpose, and the fire of your vision will always burn stronger than your fear, I can promise you that.

When you can go from a place of reacting to breathing, taking a pause, connecting in with your truth and identifying a logical, aligned response to whatever is happening, you will move out of your Survival Brain into your Alpha Creative Brain, the place where you will access your Ultramind, altered states of consciousness and divine intelligence. Creativity and attraction happen from this new part of your brain. However, accessing it requires your brainwaves to slow down.

I discovered the "Alpha Creative Brain" through breathwork.

I didn't truly get into breathwork until 2021 when I discovered Soma Breath. Up until then, breathwork was just another of the many things I tried to heal my anxiety, but to be honest, it just made me more anxious!

When I discovered Soma Breath, I was finally able to relax into the breathing techniques, and I found myself drifting off into these magical states where I would connect with visions, downloads and messages. I became hooked on my daily dose of breathwork that was not only connecting me to my inner power, truth and creativity, but helping me in my health also. I felt amazing.

I decided to invest in a 21-day Breathwork Awakening at the end of 2020, where you do a different breathwork journey each week for 3 weeks, but I got really stuck on the third week's track. It was an hour and 3 minutes long and used very fast breath rhythms from early on in the journey that made me anxious. I am literally the type of person who won't be "beaten" by anything, and I was fascinated both by the positive experience with Soma Breath and by how I was struggling so much with the Awakening.

So, I started to discover more about the Breathwork Modality and its creator, Niraj Naik, who I resonated with immediately. Niraj was a pharmacist who worked for Walmart. He used to use the little 15-minute sessions the pharmacists had to check on the customer's medication by giving the customer a consultation and helping them to reduce the medication they needed by integrating lifestyle changes. Sure enough, the customers' shopping bags were getting smaller. Walmart's profits started to suffer, and he lost his job!

Niraj's health story also resonated with me. He had been diagnosed with a supposedly incurable condition, but he took matters into his own hands to heal it, and he did! His approach reminded me of when I had been diagnosed with Hashimoto's in 2014, and I knew that I could cure it with nutrition and lifestyle changes, but the doctors didn't believe me. I proved them wrong and went into remission!

What Niraj had created in Soma Breath to create deep transformation through breathwork and music, looked phenomenal and resonated with all the ways I wanted to serve people more deeply by helping them overcome their limitations, letting go of past traumas and shifting their identity to enjoy a truly healthy, happy and limitless life of Abundance. I also LOVED the music.

Accessing your Ultramind is like returning to your childhood mind, where your brainwaves slow down into an alpha daydreamy state because there is no danger in your perspective. In an alpha brainwave state, imagination and visualisation is easy. You can create a whole new way of thinking that makes taking new empowered action easy.

You can magnify alpha brain waves using breathwork. You can access an enjoyable 22-minute gratitude breathwork at my YouTube channel.

Gratitude is also a way to access the Ultramind. Gratitude "feels good." It helps you lose the attachment to outcomes and expectations and just appreciate everything you have. It helps you see situations from a new perspective in the moment. Fear is the only thing that stops you doing this. For example, in the moments of struggle that might normally take you into your survival brain, the statement "I'm so grateful this is happening to me" will take you into your Ultramind where solutions happen.

The power of gratitude to make you take a second look at your life and turn your attention from the bad to the good is unmatched. However, like growing a muscle, gratitude takes time to develop, and you must practise it consistently.

Generally, we don't know how to expand consciousness in this way. Our imagination has been made redundant by our Survival Mind, and we are stuck in our beta brainwaves. Blocked from Alpha Creation and unable to access the Ultra-mind where we can literally bend reality.

BLOCKED FROM QUANTUM CREATION

Quantum Creation is where the Universe takes the reins. That plan I mentioned the Universe has? Set your vision, and the Universe will help you experience the most magical way to create it. You will not have to structure, manipulate or force anything at all, and this magic will be at a level you never could have matched anyway!

However, to experience this magic you have to be open to the challenges that will inevitably show up.

Life has to challenge us, but not too much. Everything is about balance. If we are not challenged, we are bored and uninspired. If we are challenged, and we have done the internal work to have empowering belief systems, we will access the Ultra-mind and find a creative solution.

Challenge gives us intel about our opportunities for growth. We should always be in search of new ways to grow. Stretching our comfort zones is the perfect way to find challenge.

However, if we are challenged too much, life becomes a struggle. Healing trauma will help you to always be in an empowered place through Challenge, so that you are never challenged too much. This is because trauma makes us believe that the outcome of the challenge, the person creating it or the challenge itself, has control over us. However, it never really does. Commit to believe that right now and give up all negative influences in your life upon your life and all negativity within yourself.

One of the most powerful affirmations I have used on my healing journey is that everything is happening around me, not to me, and I can always control how I respond. This always keeps me in my Ultramind, able to find a measured, aligned response or find the question and/or gratitude that will take me away from the negative thoughts, words and the beliefs that don't serve me. No matter what happens in life, if you view challenges through a positive lens, there is nothing that will stand in your way of success or happiness.

PRACTICAL INTEGRATION

4 TIPS TO ALWAYS BE SUPPORTED BY THE UNIVERSE, TAPPED INTO THE QUANTUM FIELD AND BE QUANTUM CREATING!

1. **Nurture your alpha brain waves,** so that you are constantly generating aligned ideas, concepts and creations. Commit to try the 22-Minute Breathwork on my YouTube channel. You can access this here. If you like it, try some of the other journeys on my channel!

2. **Be in healthy control of your emotional state** aka hack your limiting emotions! You can achieve this through trauma healing and beginning the journey of elevating your consciousness, so that you are in a state to implement new ideas, develop new strategies, strengthen the positives in your human experience, take action and manage the outcomes from your actions.

3. **Keep upgrading your identity** in line with the deepening connection you have with your truth by replacing misaligned habits and clearing emotional and physical clutter in your life. You can also eliminate negatives and weaknesses just by taking your focus away from them.

JOURNALING

What are some of the misaligned habits you can replace right now? The Money Coach I signed up with in 2021, after I worked with Niyc, used to call this **"Raising Your Standards."** He used to ask me, "Clare, how can you raise your standards?" I used to feel a fresh lease of life every time he asked me.

4. **Never look at your external reality** to confirm what is true in your heart! Believe in the truth that you want for you, and what you believe will come true!

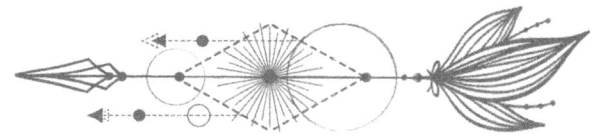

TIMELY ACTION - HEALING

*"The most important decision we make is
whether to believe we live in
a friendly or hostile universe."*
EINSTEIN

There comes a moment in your life when you have to stop running from the truth.

When you stand face to face with the uncomfortable truth that all of the issues in your life aren't the reason you don't have what you want.

And accept that the issue IS YOU.

It is what is inside you that is blocking more income coming to you, impact coming through you and abundance in your life.

If you want to attract a higher frequency life to you, it means you have to live a high frequency life and give up the behaviours and patterned reactions that are standing between you and your desired future.

It means you have to reconnect with the past in a new and different way, like I did, with forgiveness and understanding, rather than anger and regret, so you can see the deep learnings in your story and your experiences, and understand how you can change the world in the way you've always had a deep passion to do.

When you do this, your energy shifts, your heart opens and your frequency rises. Your perspectives change, your nervous system relaxes, and then your vision opens, clarity comes, ideas give birth, problems solve themselves, and you experience healing.

You start feeling wealthy and abundant, and wealth and abundance starts to come to you. You fall deeply in love with yourself and in love with life and stop feeling all bitter and twisted inside, so your body stops seeking to find the instances in your daily life that enable you to feel bitter and twisted as an expression of all the feelings that haven't been transmuted. You'll stop making things that happen in your life about you, and life will stop happening to you.

It's a hard pill to swallow, right? That everything you have and everything you have had is coming and has come from you. But if you can swallow it, it means you are ready for the timely action of healing. This moment might come in the experience of your emotions heightening so much and feeling so heavy that you feel like you are going to vomit them up. You may feel like you have become allergic to yourself and everything you are and so suddenly, change is your only option. You may feel helpless and hopeless until you remember you can feel empowered by the pull of the INTENTION we have talked about all the way through this book.

Who do you want to be?

How do you want to feel?

What do you want to believe?

What is the experience of life you want to have?

For so much time, before I finally collapsed to my knees on that food bank floor, I felt the worst kind of sadness, the type you can't explain, like an undercurrent of discontent within, which you can't really name or attribute to anything. I've mentioned it already. I call it **"The Void,"** which is like the ghosts in horror movies; its presence is unnerving, looming and ominous.

My corporate job with the flashy car and good salary hadn't filled "The Void." The love of my life and marriage hadn't filled "The Void." Having two beautiful daughters who mean more to me than anything in the world didn't fill the "The Void." And my lack of self-worth was at the centre of it, and it grew every time I had an experience that validated that I wasn't worthy.

Before timely healing, emotions create an identity that will have you acting out in ways that can never create the future of your dreams, but after timely healing, a world of opportunity opens up. Remember... **the body is the mind.** Our physical reactions come from the place of our limiting beliefs and trauma, they create the thoughts that keep us safe, and the action and inaction that flow from these survival thoughts so life stays the same. A frustrating repeat of the same struggles. We become the ripple effect of our stories, our parents' stories, maybe even our parents' parents' stories and beyond! We are a reflection of how we experience our circumstances through our emotions, which is a reflection of everything we believe.

When I chose the journey of healing, I began to feel differently about money, and I made more money. I started to become more positive and push everything in my life that didn't reflect my values out, which upleveled all of my experiences and relationships. I began aligning my life to the things I loved, I started contributing my time to the things and people that brought me joy, and applying my heart and passion to everything I was discovering about myself and the person I wanted to become. As I did this, I became more successful. As I began to walk proudly more aligned to myself, my personal brand burned brighter than any paid support could have ever masterminded, and my business started to shift. More importantly, my life filled with colour, fulfilment, and enjoyment.

This healing was timely because I chose it. I had no resistance to it, and I was connected to my inner truth.

In this energy and in my willingness to invest in support, my financial abundance shifted. In some metaphysical way, it was like I'd needed to resettle the balance that had been out of whack for so long by me holding onto money and being scared to spend it. I went from spending nothing to spending heaps! Hundreds of thousands of dollars. And then the balance tipped the other way. The Universe began to show me multiple ways to get support for free.

It was crazy. It was like there had always been this unspoken law that balance will always prevail and that the Universe will always support your goals when you support the balance.

After you begin the process of healing your internal condition, you will "need" for nothing but be open to everything; in true belief in yourself and your energetic channels of abundance, you will be wide open to receive everything you desire.

A client of mine, after our coaching together for a few weeks, said that she was finally able to look back on a past that had tortured her like a storybook. She could see the pictures, what had gone before, but wasn't any longer overwhelmed by the emotions like she once had been.

Healing is like that. The pictures we were once so afraid to look at change.

I had a memory come back to me in a retreat once, of my dad coming home late from work, where I ran at his legs as he came through the front door and embraced them.

The funny thing is that I had been guided to remember a negative association to money. Knowing how to move into an altered state of consciousness fast with my breath and let go of the logical mind, I allowed my subconscious mind to gift me the memory I was re-experiencing without question.

As I watched my child self run to my dad and embrace him, I realised a limiting belief I had and why my income had plateaued in that moment. Because my dad worked so hard and so late, I believed that money equalled absence. I was resisting making more money because I was unconsciously believing that more money would come at the sacrifice of time with my children.

Resistance is physical. We feel a lack of motivation and inertia in our body. The body sabotages us in creative ways. Something I see often in my clients is how the BODY comes in and gate-crashes the NEW INCOME. I create FAST results for my clients. We can break 5 figures in as little as 4 weeks! And what often comes after this is illness.

Old injuries flaring, autoimmune issues coming up, a massive flu or other virus, or just epic fatigue.

Starting to see the body's clever ways of sabotaging your progress will stop you from hitting income plateaus!

Many will not realise they need to work through trauma as part of their business strategy, especially not the trauma held in the cell memory of their body.

Many will try to work through their trauma in their mind only and not know to bring the body along the journey.

But as you know now, the body doesn't forget your experiences.

Triggers will cause your sympathetic nervous system to unconsciously switch on and trigger a survival response without you being consciously aware of it. For example, I made money and then pulled back, felt resistance, and subconsciously sabotaged more income with inaction. Because the presence of money triggered the unconscious belief that making more would lead to me being absent from my children like Dad was absent from me.

Your limiting beliefs don't have to be logical. If you are experiencing an income ceiling, or if you feel your body SHUDDER at the thought that you need to invest more time to create more money, or if your own body has a pattern of shutting down on you after launches or when you push hard in your business, these are all good indications that you might have trauma to clear.

I worked with another client who created rapid success and fast money in her business after struggling to make money at all and then she found herself struggling to post social media content.

When she brought this up in a session, we worked through my **Lens Process**, which is a multidimensional, neurosomatic trauma release therapy and identified what was coming up from her past. We cleared it, so she could step fully into the identity of the success she had created in her UNLEASHED Vision and the success she wanted to expand and create more of.

Basically.... We freed her up to make MORE MONEY!

I always get flooded with content to express when I am in flow and feeling good. I call this the "**content waterfall**." However, stress, overthinking, and confusion all block my connection to that flow. I call this the "**content dam**."

I have noticed self-care is paramount to this flow, and I had to redefine what self-care meant to me to be able to maintain it.

Rather than it being something I did occasionally to make me feel a temporary lift to a chronic low with bath salts and rose petals, self-care became the things I do every day to empower freedom from the things that were leaving me exhausted, frustrated or overwhelmed.

This is why I will always advocate for transformational coaching as a vehicle for making money. I know for me, personally, a 15-minute meditation is worth much more than marketing strategy because it reconnects me to myself and my Soul Goal, and that is where my best content and solutions lie. I have had 5 figure days from the simplest of content that has come straight out of my morning meditation!

In altered states of consciousness, where the survival mind switches off and the Ultramind opens up, we are most aligned to who we really are in our truth and how we want to live our lives. In living from this place, we feel happiness. This high frequency allows us to sail through whatever life throws at us. You can start to establish this self connection today by letting go of the things that don't bring you joy and investing only in the things that bring colour to your life, more potency, and more promise. Reconnect to your Joy GPS Journal and ask yourself where you can carve in more of the activities that make you feel joyful. Then, commit to keep letting go of what doesn't make you happy and hold on with unrelenting gratitude for everything that does.

Gratitude unlocks the fullness of life. We can always give thanks, even in the darkest of times. When my mum was diagnosed with breast cancer, I gave thanks that I had hands and a mobile phone, and I picked the damn thing up and made a phone call that I had been putting off for the better part of a year. In 2018, both my friend and my sister-in-law had received the news that their breast cancer was at stage 4 and had become metastatic. My heart broke at the news of this. They were both a similar age to me with half a lifetime ahead of them. They both had children, and they were both beautiful people.

I decided to organise a Sponsored Burpee to generate money, as both my sister-in-law and friend were not working. I pledged to do 500 burpees to fundraise because it was something that I felt was impossible to achieve (I caved at 50 burpees usually) and I made contact with the local Breast Cancer service in my town and offered to try and raise money and awareness for them too. When I went to speak to them about this, I was overwhelmed by the work they do for the women in our local area who are suffering with breast cancer. I came away wanting to help them more, but my scarcity mindset talked me out of it. Who was I to become a sponsor of a charity like that? What could I give? My business was hardly sustainable! Reeling from the news about my mum, I called them with gratitude for everything I could give and offered to give it. Workshops, talks, one of my online courses. I had a whole new perspective of the value I could add. The following week, another friend lost her battle to breast cancer and she had so much life left to live. If I could help other women to live every day of their lives to its maximum potential, that was a gift worth giving.

PRACTICAL INTEGRATION

There are two other tools that are staples with my clients.

1.   The Give to Gain Tool
2.   Anchors

I invite you to try these tools out. You can find resources at my website, https://clare-williamson.com/home-6592

SECTION 3

THE "HOW"

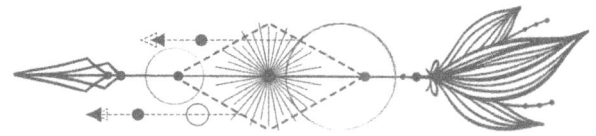

CAN YOU HANDLE THE TRUTH?

*I*n a retreat in 2020, I stared into the eyes of one of the most beautiful girls I have ever seen, and while holding her hands, I realised how the only other eyes I had held in an unbroken gaze like this for more than a millisecond since the rape were the eyes of my own children.

I broke down into tears.

How could I have lived for so long with so little trust of people who could have been so innocent and beautiful just like this? How many relationships had I passed up the opportunity to have because I didn't trust people?

There is a part in the film, *A Few Good Men*, where he shouts, "You can't handle the truth!" And it is true.

It is confronting the truth that your world is just a construct from your programming. As you begin to know yourself, know your power and follow your inner compass, there will be many areas of life where you question what you have always believed. You will feel anxiety and fear, just like I did, as you exit your own Matrix and deconstruct the fabric of your world.

You end up in this nowhere place.

Yet how wonderful to see your world through the lens of your authentic truth, trust and unconditional love because you are still in your deep healing journey, but unable to go back to a world built out of the beliefs you had.

You'll realise that even your gut instinct has been wrong in the past and see where it was also framed by your limiting beliefs and your scarcity mindset.

You will be unsure about trusting yourself for a little while and this will affect how you are able to be in complete flow with whatever happens as you take this journey of true healing, growth and raising consciousness. This is where having a Coach who has walked the path before you is so powerful to help you trust that everything is happening on purpose and this journey is part of the magic key to you finally living in abundance because it activates your creative power.

To access the creativity that takes your income and impact to the next level, you must learn to slow down your brain waves and quiet the default mode of your mind despite the fear and anxiety you feel.

You have to learn to focus with clear intent and hold onto the good feelings of what you want. And you must trust that you can have all of what you want and that it can happen easily.

When my business started to pop in 2020, it was because I created a #personalstoryformula to explode my leads on social media. A big part of it being successful for you is trusting that it can be done in just an hour a day and ditch the hustle paradigm. We are not taught that things can be easy like this. We are taught that hard work pays dividends. From early childhood, we are being assessed, compared and rewarded for our work efforts. Work efforts guarantee a pay cheque. If we work harder, we get paid more.

I had a memory surface once during a healing session. I had been struggling to launch a new product, a Mastermind, and I could feel in my heart what I wanted it to be, but I couldn't see a clear vision of it and my block was stopping me from moving forward and creating it. It was like when I tried to look forward, I felt a dark, heavy cloud just behind me to my right, and it would feel like it was swallowing me up, and I would get this hopeless feeling that I couldn't overcome, which would rob me of my motivation to work on anything Mastermind related. I just kept finding myself with excuses and procrastination.

In the healing session, my subconscious mind guided me back to a time when I was in my mid-teens, reading a letter from my parents. We had been having difficulties, and I had gone to live with a friend from school. Julia, actually, one of the first girls I had met when I moved to my new school after Dad lost his business.

When I opened the letter, I'd had hopes in my heart that Mum and Dad were offering an olive branch. I wanted to go home, but my relationship with them was struggling. I pulled the letter out of its envelope and began to read. My heart dropped with each line. The letter went into great detail about how the situation was all up to me and how I was "difficult, selfish, and I needed to change."

As I remembered the letter and the feeling in my body, my mind started to drift to another memory, only it felt like it wasn't mine. I was in what seemed like a big dark box with lots of other boys my age. I was around 14 or 15 and I was looking at myself and wondering how to be in my new clothes and new hair. In my right hand, I held the only thing that still felt like me, a wooden yo-yo with my name scratched on it... William. Only I'd forgotten the "i" in my name and it sat above my name. It looked so personal to me. As I was looking at it, someone took it out of my hand and said, "You won't be needing that where you are going, George." I looked at them as they swapped out my yo-yo for a wooden staff and filed me in a line behind the other boys. They hadn't only changed my name, they had washed me, brushed my hair, cut me a fringe, and changed my clothes. I was a shadow of the old me, who was far more interested in moving and creating than washing and keeping clean.

As the line of boys filed forward, each boy in a white tunic with a burgundy sash and a wooden staff, I realised I had been in a shipping box, and we were walking out to the port. To the right, just behind me stood a crowd of people, thick with noise, some jeering, some supporting. I scanned the crowd, looking for an escape. It felt like if I kept marching forward in the direction of the other boys, I would never be able to be the true me again. But there was no way through the crowd that I could see, so I kept walking.

As my subconscious mind drifted out of William's memory, realising its gift of knowing my role to close the loop on this block to authentic, creative expression, I understood why I'd been so blocked and repeated William's fate of inexpression. I was back in my own body, holding my mum and dad's letter and feeling that intense "fundamentally flawed" feeling to the core of me. Deep shame. I was ashamed of who I was authentically and terrified of my own creative expression. I felt like the thing on the production line that gets chucked off. The reject.

The tears started to stream, and it felt like there was an ocean of them to come. It felt like the gush of tears was finally moving and releasing the thick feeling of shame about who I was. I allowed my subconscious mind to drift back to William in his truth. I saw through his eyes looking at the path forward where he knew he could never express himself authentically again, where he would be fated to a life of conformity.

And I saw the crowd of people to his right, but this time I felt his freedom to run. I felt him drop his staff and rip off his sash and burst into a run. I felt him put his head down and forge his own path through the crowd and then as his memory drifted away from mine, I saw him from a distance, sit on a tree stump, scratching his name into a new yo-yo and choosing to place the "i" differently, as his own personal signature. I felt the beauty of creation in William's peace and smile, and I felt the intention to make my Mastermind whatever the hell I wanted it to be. I realised that despite how I'd felt like I'd gotten it wrong so many times in childhood, there was no such thing as right or wrong. Only other people's beliefs that we can choose to be a victim to or not.

It's easier to give up our power, than face the discomfort of all the things we believe about ourselves before we finally find freedom from them. Powerlessness is the core state of most people who haven't begun their journey of self-healing. It causes them to consistently look outside of themselves for fixes to the issues they manifest from their own victim consciousness, and then they'll often blame something outside of themselves when the solution they try doesn't work. Again, it's easier not to take responsibility because deep down this satisfies their limiting beliefs about themselves. And society supports this victim mentality believe it or not.

I heard a great podcast where the guy called it the "Victim Olympics," where everyone is competing to be the biggest victim and society celebrates it with all the systems set up to give people handouts and compensation. Part of my "step out of the Matrix" was realising that this is where governments need us—powerless and in fear. I was like... "You mean all of these things I thought were keeping me safe were just an illusion?"

For a moment, I couldn't handle the truth. I saw how the health system is really just there to make us sicker, and I felt let down and angry. I heard that doctors get about 5 minutes training on the true superpowers of the human body to heal itself simply with nature. I grieved the false sense of safety and security I'd had and feared the "nowhere place" I found myself in. However, now I know that to awaken your Miracle Frequency and have it all, easily, you have to realise your own power and unleash your freedom of choice and creativity. Otherwise, you will always just be a robot to other people's beliefs.

Remember... the energy of fear will manifest more of what you fear.

And if you can remove fear from your life, you will manifest a beautiful, exhilarating and abundant life easily.

Revisit your pledge to turn your life around. Slip into deeper intention to find your power, unleash your creativity and reclaim your freedom of choice.

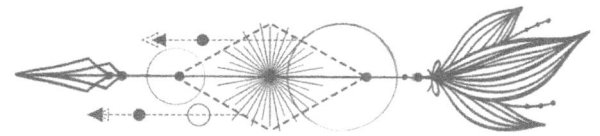

PURIFICATION

Before you begin your life change, I am going to invite you to make another life-changing decision, based on another game-changing truth.

You can't think good thoughts if your body doesn't feel good.

As we travelled around Mexico in 2023 and were initially limited in our local knowledge as to where to find the markets for fresh fruit and veggies, we made some bad food choices. I felt it in my body because I felt horrible.

In 2019, I made the decision to start treating my body better. We'd been trying to have my third baby. Craig and I had three miscarriages trying. I was devastated, but it was my body screaming to be looked after better. I was training five days a week, twice a day. I wanted a Muay Thai title, but my body was suffering. My coach had found me a match for a title fight, but my doctor told me I shouldn't fight it and referred me for a colonoscopy to eliminate the chance I had cancer in my bowels because I was bleeding when I went to the toilet. I looked terrible. I'd lost a heap of weight, and I just knew something had to change.

I connected with another network marketing company that offered superfood powders and completely clean products. They were running a 30-day detox, and I signed up! Within 30 days, I felt incredible. I then became pregnant with Bowie, and she is still here with us today.

Purification is now something I do daily. This is a short chapter, but I felt it was important to share with you the simple things you can do daily to support your body and open your energetic channels of abundance. This is something we focus significantly on in my programmes and those who will not visit the area of their health will generally experience more plateaus in their income than those who will.

I can't say I fully understand it, but I see it, and I've learned to pay attention to patterns like this. As I have just shared, I don't believe the world as we have been sold it—the Matrix we were plugged into from the moment we were born and given a name—is as the world truly is. I believe the human body is superhuman. I feel a connection to the spirit in everything and that the human body is in beautiful flow with the energy of nature. I believe the body's cells benefit from the things that are ingested as nature intended. I believe the human mind holds magical powers, and I believe in a world of opportunity and abundance if we can come back to the true nature of ourselves and our superpowers.

PRACTICAL INTEGRATION

Before you take the steps I share with you later in the book, which will help you crack your Abundance Code and transform your life, it is important to open your energetic channels to prosperity. You can do this with the following steps:

- Reduce your coffee intake to no more than one cup a day
- Invest in a good probiotic and consider introducing colostrum as a supplement. I have links to the ones I trust at my website (www.themillionaireshawoman.com)
- Increase your water intake to 3 litres a day

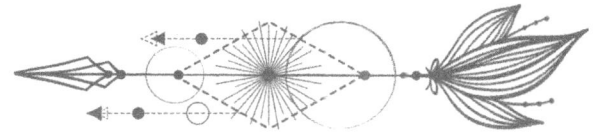

LIVING MY LIFE IN RITUAL

On November 10, 2021, my life changed unrecognizably. My business had hit new heights. I'd finally hit the infamous six-figure accolade!!!! I had clients, influence and was busy. My Mastermind was launched and a success, but I was also still coaching 1:1 but I was now a mum of three and Bowie now had some health issues. We'd had a period of illness with her that had led to her recovering, but gave up sleeping in the process.

I soldiered on through the tiredness. I could feel that the administrative work that my high client base created was an energy leak, but I'd not found administrative support by that point that had really taken the pressure off. (I now know a big part of this was my lack of systems and communication.) I could feel myself "cruising" in my business. I'd lost the spark for what I was doing as the promise of my #personalstory-formula to transform how you use social media and generate leads was calling in people who wanted visibility, without the deep transformation work it takes to push through the visibility ceilings that come from the inside.

In between the chaos, I would find magical moments of flow. I was using the somatic movement, neurosomatic breathwork and other techniques I had learned in the course I'd started earlier that year and starting to love all of it. However, it always came second priority to my business.

While I was still sticking to my one hour a day social media strategy, my hours on the admin side of my business had started to creep up, and I was often coaching 10-15 hours a week and taking sales calls on top of that. I'd also taken on a Positive Psychology certification that I'd fallen behind with when Bowie got sick, so I was also redoing the whole programme and trying to get my final assessment together.

It was like any other day. It was Bowie's childcare day, so I dropped the kids at school and then her to day-care. I had a hundred things on my mind, and I know I was turning them over as I got out of the car and went into the house. When I came back out to pick the kids up, I noticed condensation on the window of the car. I pulled open the door and found my beautiful dog slumped on the driver's seat.

I screamed and fell to my knees, the words circling through my screams, "No, what have I done, my boy!" I couldn't move through the pain that ran through my body, and I couldn't see through my eyes. I dragged myself up to my neighbour's house screaming for help. He couldn't make sense out of me when he opened the door and then someone I didn't know was there trying to calm me down.

Some days I feel like those moments are frozen in time. They replay slowly in my mind, and I still can't understand them. I still don't know why Benson (Benny) was in the car. He came everywhere with me, but as a Bernese Mountain Dog, as big as a horse, he always jumped up in the back when we parked, ready to jump out when we arrived home.

A part of me died with Benny that day, but in a good way. Even still, for days after it happened, I wanted Spirit to take me as well. Every day was a blur and a rollercoaster of emotions between disbelief and feeling the most gut-wrenching guilt and I didn't know how I would get through it. Every time I closed my eyes I saw him, laying there lifeless on the car seat. No amount of trying to cry out the pain, curled into the fetal position would cry the pain away. I felt hopeless. I kept trying to play out the moments leading up to finding him, the months before, the days before, the day it happened. Nothing led me to really know why I didn't know he was in the car.

A few days after we lost him, one of my own Quantum Coaches (I had created a *Quantum Coaching Certificate* by this point) reached out to me and said the words I needed to hear to save me from myself. She said, "You have the tools to get yourself through this, Clare." At first, it was like she was speaking a foreign language. I knew she was talking to me, but I couldn't quite grasp what she was saying. She dug in further, "Clare, this is where you help other people, you can get yourself through this."

I hung up the call and lay with her words. She had shifted my perspective from this tragedy happening to me, to through me, and I felt glimmers of my own power through the pain. The next morning, I locked myself away in my office and I opened Microsoft Word. My hand hovered over the keyboard. One of the activities I have my coaches do for their certification is write an "Integration Plan" and it's where they have to take everything they know and take it into a written plan that helps them to achieve the outcome they are seeking.

I started there. What was the vision I was seeking? It was like I was back to that question that Lesley had asked me all those years ago... "If you don't want this, Clare, what do you want?" Only now it wasn't a scarcity of money that was uncomfortable, it was a scarcity of time. My business had become this rope around my neck, and I was close to hanging myself on it. I had created a monster. A vehicle to the income I wanted, but at the sacrifice of what? And I knew that what I had created was nothing else but a manifestation of my own belief systems, so what was I carrying in my energetic blueprint that had led me to manifest what I did? I knew I didn't need to understand that yet, but I needed to see the patterns that had created the situation I had:

- The pattern of putting my clients first
- The pattern of saying yes too often
- The pattern of running until I dropped

(These were just a few!)

The fastest and easiest way to change a pattern of habit that isn't serving you is to create a new rhythm that enforces the new pattern or habit you want. It's like if you buy a gym membership and intend to go whenever you want, your inertia may win over your intention and you won't go, but if you buy a gym membership, commit to a class and then build the class into your daily rhythm, you are more likely to go. And going consistently is so important because you begin to create a positive emotional association to the activity, where previously there might have been a negative one. I know I experienced this with giving up drinking every day and taking up daily breathwork. I started to crave the effects of breathwork like I'd used to crave the effects of alcohol. I recognized how good I felt after breathwork, I remembered how bad I felt after drinking and I began to consistently choose feeling good over whatever instant gratification my body was seeking.

Because there is another choice—instant gratification or long-term happiness and healthiness?

Often the feelings we crave—the buzz of an alcoholic drink, the feelings of connection from a sexual encounter, the lift of coffee are an indulgence of a feeling we crave or a distraction from a feeling we want to avoid. They are short-term gratifications. Whereas long-term happiness and healthiness comes from abstaining from short-term gains, so the feelings we experience give us the messages we need to understand our indulgence or distraction.

The old me would have written myself off with alcohol after Benny died. Instead, I met and experienced every difficult and gut-wrenching emotion and because I did, as I began to write my Integration Plan, I could see the rhythm I needed to create to break the patterns that I had.

I needed to create space. The thing about having it is that it brings up all your deepest, darkest desires and fears, but I was ready for the discomfort. Benson's sacrifice couldn't be for nothing. I committed my life to ritual. Waking with a morning ritual, dropping into ritual after I'd dropped the kids off at school, again before lunch, again before school pick-up, again a little after school pick-up, after dinner and a little before falling asleep.

"Ritual" simply meant opening a sacred space and dropping into breathwork, prayer, movement or gratitude. Anything that broke me away from the "real world," slowed my brainwaves down, brought my heart and mind into coherence and allowed me to drift away. I was amazed at what started to happen, really fast. In spite of what had happened with Benson, my spirits started to lift. I felt deeply connected with my purpose and flooded with creative ideas. Even though I had pulled right back from my business by only doing my "DMO" on social media (the thing I built my #personalstoryformula around), anything that felt inspired and the minimum amount of hours I could get away with in terms of admin, opportunities and clients were still coming to me. It was almost like, energetically I was saying... you know what? I've said I trust you, Universe, and now I am going to prove it.

I am held

I am divinely supported

Everything in my life is in flow

These were affirmations I used every day and for the first time ever, because my action matched them, I felt their truth and power in my body.

I was creating neuroplasticity.

What is happening when we try to reprogramme our subconscious mind with affirmations we don't truly believe, is that our action plays out completely the opposite. We unconsciously shift back to the default patterns of our core beliefs.

Money is scarce

I am unsafe

Working creates security

No neuroplasticity. We automatically latch onto the to-do list, fail to prioritise ourselves, feel stress and react to our circumstances and unconsciously continue to create a life that never changes.

One of my Soma Breath mentors suggested on a call once that Benson was my Jesus. He told a story of how it had taken the death of his mother to commit to changing his health. In spite of owning a successful chain of yoga studios and leading a brand founded in wellbeing, he was drinking too much, partying too hard and disrespecting his body. I think his mum had an underlying illness, and he found her dead on her kitchen floor. He said that he felt she had sacrificed her life for him to save his own and that Benson had done the same for me.

This idea confronted me in my guilt of how he had passed, but I believe in co-creation. I could already see how in every passing—human or animal—involving another there is a crazy spiralling of actions. A co-creation of "in the moment" decisions that lead to the intertwining of destinies. And on both sides, there is intention in energy that the Universe can only say yes to. My energy was screaming, "I'm done, I'm at capacity, I can't take anymore" and I believe Benson's energy was screaming the same.

He was tired. His body was ailing. And he had never found peace on this human plane. He had always been anxious. We had never been able to fully settle it. He was so loved, we walked him daily, fed him raw food, did everything you are supposed to do, but there was always this look in his eyes that seemed to say.... I am not sure what I am doing here, will you help me?

About three months before he passed, he started doing strange things. My neighbour had to get out of her car and physically move him out of the road because he was just sitting there in some sort of trance as she had pulled up and tried to turn into our shared driveway. He had also collapsed close to our house. I had to lift him—45+ kilos—and carry him 100m to the boot of my car just so I could take him to the vet.

I was terrified. I was so worried there was something wrong, but they couldn't find anything obvious. A couple of nights before he passed, he slipped out of his collar while we were walking and ran home. That night he was an anxious mess. I was trying to get the kids to bed, and he was stuck to me like Velcro. I kept tripping over him, and he was drooling everywhere. I snapped at him. I said, "For goodness' sake Benson, you would be better off dead than anxious like this all the time!" I hated myself for such a long time after he had gone for saying this. I wished I could take it back and hold the memory of telling him how much I loved him instead because I did. I loved him like a child. I would never have left him in that car on purpose.

But a co-creation of moments led to those final moments. I didn't see him in the rear-view mirror like I always did. He didn't jump up and shake the car like he always did, and I didn't see his big panting face. It didn't trigger my usual pattern of opening the boot and taking him inside with me. Was he sleeping? Was he not feeling well? I will never know. One of the most punishing things is that on that day he was in the car dying, I felt "in flow." I benefited from the peace and quiet from the children, I relaxed, I got into my tasks. I didn't hear him bark. Nothing felt different than any other day until I opened the door to my car and saw him lying there and knew I would never be able to "unsee" again.

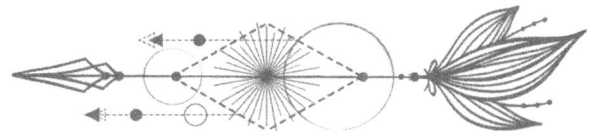

WHAT IF YOUR REPTILIAN BRAIN IS YOUR GREATEST ALLY?

"When you put creativity into everything, everything becomes available to you."
~ ROBERT RODRIGUEZ

I've talked about your reptilian brain and its negative part of the survival response that takes you away from your truth, and right now, it may feel somewhat of an enemy to your progress.

However, it is not necessarily the enemy you think. Your subconscious mind holds your power to shift your identity, so you can experience the success and abundance you want because as well as being part of your survival response, it is also your access to super-sensory capacities and radically deepened perceptual ability and thus impenetrable protection from everything you have previously feared and ancient wisdom that will unlock your powers of magnetic attraction.

Your Reptilian Brain is part of accessing your Ultramind and awakening your Miracle Frequency, so you can have it all and it can be easy. We get so broken by the experiences we have had to overcome that we forget that when we can transcend the emotion of them, we are left with wisdom that changes our world.

I battled the "scars of flow" after Benson because it felt impossible to trust that I was safe in the moment to let go. I suffered from obsessive "checking." I'd check the car was empty multiple times a day or I'd feel panic in random places like the supermarket or gym that one of the children hadn't gotten out of the car at school drop-off.

I remember going into a full panic attack one day in the gym fully believing that my middle child was in the car. I couldn't find the memory of her getting out of the car at school. What if she had hidden behind the seat as a game? It was hot, and I was seeing terrifying visions of her dying in her car seat. It was completely ridiculous and irrational, but not in my mind and body. I ran like a crazy woman and then upon finding the car empty, I sat in my hot car and cried. I left the windows up and felt the temperature of the car rising. I forced myself to feel what Benson must have felt until I couldn't take it anymore, and I had to open the windows.

I took to leaving the car windows down all the time after that. I would text Craig to make sure all the kids got out of the car when he did the drop-off. I found it so hard to relax, but I used breathwork and continued to drop into ritual seven times a day. Gradually, things got easier.

In ritual, as I inhaled and lifted my mind out of my body, I was able to observe the emotions that sat there. The fear, the anxiety and the grief. As I exhaled, I'd see now some of what I'd noticed would just release itself from me. I started to realise I was none of those feelings—the guilt, the self-hate, the sadness or the fear—I was just the observer of them. This opened up this incredible spaciousness. I'd feel myself suspended in "the space" and yet so beautifully connected to the truth of myself in energy, and the more I dropped into this space through ritual, the more the darkness disappeared, and I could see and feel the light. I felt clear and intentional. I felt on purpose. It was like I remembered my purpose. I found my inner fire!!

It was January, and everyone around me in my business circle was making plans and adopting strategies for the new year. I had a sudden startle and thought, "Holy shit, where have I been? Isn't this what I also do every year? Isn't this how I have been successful?" I renewed my membership with my business coach for another six months and organised our strategic call.

Across nearly two hours we planned out the next six months of launches. If I wanted to make one million dollars this year, this was how it could happen. Starting with rinsing and repeating my successful Challenge, *UNLEASH Your Legacy*, which showed people how to use my #personalstoryformula as a vehicle to attract leads online and fully step into their soul goal. The challenge ran in February and was, as usual, a success, despite me completely losing my voice on the second day and having to do the challenge a little differently. I signed up four clients, but I felt flat. They were far from the expansion I felt in my soul (expansion was my word for the year!) They just wanted to make a shift in their social media and make some money. I took their non-refundable deposits and started their onboarding. And then they ALL pulled out! I sat with this for a while and tried not to feel the failure and the fear in it. I tried to take the message in the chaos that this wasn't the aligned path, even though I couldn't see what the aligned path forward was, but all I felt was this indescribable urge to play bigger and make the difference that was truly my soul goal. I recorded a YouTube video committing to giving up my own excuses to doing this. Finally, there was no going back.

And yet I struggled against the nature of my prehistoric brain; it craved the comfort of the familiar. It wanted to be sure I had a plan. It resisted the unknown of this new way, this new business I was stepping into without a brand, not really knowing who I wanted to serve and how. And things were feeling scary financially. I had invested $50K into coaching at the beginning of the year and hired a nanny so I could have my youngest at home. I didn't want to take on new clients until I felt sure about who I wanted to serve and what I wanted my business to look like, so I didn't have new sales coming in like I'd had.

Thankfully, "strange" things were happening in my financial world. In February, we received a five-figure legacy payment that matched the amount I had asked for in sales before the Challenge. Expenses in my life and business mysteriously disappeared, and I started to be offered easy, affiliate opportunities to make money. It was like the Universe was supporting my pause to go back to the drawing board and pivot my business to something more aligned and powerful, and yet I felt scared like the rug was going to be pulled out from under me at any moment. I was experiencing first-hand how the brain struggles to hold the realities of our toxic neural networks created from our limiting beliefs of the past and the visions of our future at the same time.

Then I got Covid.

It was crazy. I was completely bedridden for five whole days. I couldn't "do" anything. On day two, I felt mastitis coming on in my breast. What the hell? I didn't want to take antibiotics. I felt certain that it was connected somehow to the Universe striking me out with Covid too. I was being forced to pause. The breast is symbolically the connection to our mother. Illness in the breast is symbolic of the "Mother Wound." When I had opened the car door that day and found Benson slumped over in my car seat, I had this sickening "remembering" of how this was just another way "I get everything wrong and make bad decisions." It brought my feeling of being fundamentally flawed and broken right up to the surface. And part of what I was doing in ritual was remembering the truth of myself and healing that limiting belief, and I believe that was finally why everything else was seeming to happen for me so easily now.

My whole frequency had changed in this healing and shifted perception. As I was stepping out of the "Matrix" onto a beautiful, new, and mystical path, I was allowing the "pinprick" of light I'd been able to find in the days after Benson to take me deeper and deeper into myself, so that I could realise and embody all the qualities of my being. However, I'd also been trying to force more light to come through the tiny gap from a place of impatience, created by feeling frustrated and anxious that I couldn't see a clear picture of what was coming and that felt uncomfortable and unsafe.

Then, when I had Covid, when all I could do was lie in the space, when my husband took the kids so there was no distraction, when I invested hours and hours into going deep into myself, and asking the light to show more of itself, I finally saw the vision I had been trying so hard to see.

And I also saw what had really been blocking it.

"The brain struggles to hold the realities of our toxic neural networks created from our limiting beliefs of the past and the visions of our future at the same time."

I realised I still judged my mum for her brokenness, and I was seeing other people and other things as broken through this consciousness. And I still resented her. These toxic emotions were as damaging as the anger and resentment I'd felt about myself for what I had done to Benson. I'd forgiven myself for Benson and in doing so, erased the neural networks of these emotions in my limbic brain, but I was still hating on my mum when my lesson from Benson was UNCONDITIONAL LOVE, the ability to love everything and every person without judgement, and treasure every moment without judgement as well.

In an event earlier in the year, I had visualised my mum as a little child and seen her for the truth of what she was ... a little girl who never felt loved enough to believe she wasn't broken and a burden, and she never got to heal this limiting belief. This new perspective had set me free from my own. My ego had begun to get quiet, I stopped being quiet, and I felt more at ease with the idea of being wrong and had stopped seeing others as having more authority. As I'd begun to see differently, I began to love differently and gave myself permission to celebrate all of who I am and the fact that I can be a unique expression of my gifts.

In my raging Covid fever, as I connected with the lack of forgiveness of my mum, I encouraged myself to see her in true, unconditional love. And as I did, I saw this explosion of golden light bursting from my breast in my visualisation, and I felt the block in my breast clear and the throbbing start to subside.

The feeling of love for my mum was intense. When we create new feelings in this way, we create chemical reactions that directly impact the way we memorise and act.

The weekend after I had Covid I made the spontaneous decision to jump on an event with Derek Rydall, my previous Abundance Coach that I'd worked with, and he described the torture of where I had been the last few months without the inner sight that Covid had gifted me, which changed how I felt so radically.

"Like not being fully dead and not being fully alive."

His words shook the core of me. It had felt like I'd been in some midway place since losing Benson, and it was because I was trying to hold two conflicting realities at the same time—what I wanted to believe and what I believed. It had been creating a gap. I realised there was no gap when I can be fully in the present moment where everything is TRUTH. Derek asked me to feel my anxious feelings and truly listen to them, and I understood how they were the urgency I had been feeling to act from a misaligned place because I was still looking at the whole world like I looked at my mum. Like it needed to be fixed. I saw how there was nothing to fix.

In this even deeper enlightenment, I began to find the words I needed to wrap around the truth that had been emerging from me over so many months as I had committed daily to my rituals that had been waking up this ancient wisdom in my body and connecting me to the very core of myself and so much more deeply to my Source. My growing feeling of being part of something greater than myself was deepening my trust in divine intervention and encouraging me to say yes more and more to my Soul Goal, even if it felt like I was riding a wave of chaos. I was seeing how that was the nature of creation.

Following Covid and Derek's event, my husband and I finalised our plans to travel that December. I even started looking for venues in Tulum, Mexico for my first in-person retreat. I literally got the internal shakes and butterflies to think about it. And I realised that is how I have always wanted to live my life!

If you can change your perception, you can change your entire reality instantly. Perception is the magic that changes your reality, even when nothing in your reality changes. Remember, we create emotions in the moment. "An emotion is your brain's creation of what your bodily sensations mean, in relation to what is going on around you in the world," said Lisa Feldman Barrett.

PRACTICAL INTEGRATION

Here is an example you can practise. Wake up tomorrow and focus on the silence that surrounds you and how grateful you are that you have opened your eyes to live another day. As you run the tap to brush your teeth, focus on the shape and sparkle of the water and hear the sound of the running water deeply. Take your morning coffee outside and listen to the birds and their morning song. As thoughts float in to distract you from your focus, acknowledge them and then discard them and go back to the sounds of the song. As you make your breakfast, put your radio on and dance like no one is watching. Celebrate everything you have and everything you are yet to have and feel the warmth of your gratitude for it. As you dress the kids, play with them, make them laugh and laugh with them. As you hit a red traffic light on the way to work, instead of worrying about the consequences of being late, smile and believe everything is working out for you and enjoy the break in your drive with your grateful heart.

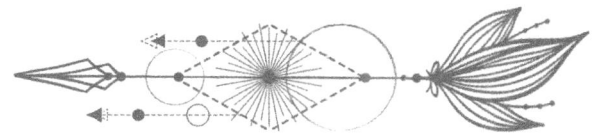

THE DAY I HEARD THE CALL

"You don't find light by avoiding the darkness."
S. KELLEY HARRELL

They say "the call" comes after your Dark Night of the Soul...

In the weeks that followed me having Covid, it felt like a big hole opened up and swallowed me. It felt like I was being called to stand deep in every single shadow of my life and business so that I could see all the broken parts that still needed healing and evolving. The urgency to complete this Transformation Cycle now felt intense.

It had been less than a year since I had broken the exhausting illusion that I was living because of deeply rooted and unresolved beliefs and seen how easy it is to get locked into the game of the ego that steals away the chance to live truly authentically and in freedom. In this time, I had remembered who I am. I had acknowledged who I am. I had started to find my voice and reclaim my power. And now it was time for the old to completely die for the new to truly birth itself.

In August, I felt an overwhelming urge to call time on the coaching I was receiving 1:1 with my Money Coach. I began to see glimmers of light, and I felt like a new journey was beckoning me, but I didn't know what it was yet. Since Covid, I'd been getting downloads in my breathworks. Messages or "intel" as it were, but I couldn't fully understand it. So, I asked to be shown the new brand of my business, and I got "The Millionaire Sha'Woman." This was so wildly different to my current brand that I almost laughed it off! Yet, I couldn't let it go either. It felt like it brought together my past, my present and my future in spirituality, oneness, and light, and it felt magical.

I couldn't share this brand with anyone. And then in one of my breathworks, the room filled with animals around me, and I was shoulder to shoulder with a gorilla, a hummingbird, a jaguar and more. They said, "It's time, Clare, we have waited long enough," and I knew they were right.

It was like the earth was calling me home. A part of myself that I had lost touch with was calling me to reconnect. My reconnection to unconditional love, through my mum, was drawing me to be more intentional in my life—in my business, as a mother—be even more present, feminine and nurturing.

I felt so creatively inspired, in trust and strong. Like there was a firm rod that ran through the centre of me and then ran down to the centre of the earth. I felt grounded and unbreakable. I could feel how I was more grounded in any situation. My old reactions no longer had a place in my body. If I felt disconnected, lost or misaligned, I no longer looked outside of myself for resolution, I simply connected more deeply within.

There is a blessing in the dark night of the soul... And it is freedom.

One day in October, I pulled a tarot card. I pulled out the "Black Egg," the symbol of opening the throat Chakra and taking hold of the truth with bravery. I felt my rebirth. I heard the call from lifetimes ago to step onto the Shaman's path. To face the rites of passage that would wake my lion's heart fully. I saw my inner Shaman in the truth that dark and light—death and rebirth—are constantly interchanging. I accepted my path as a Healer, a Lightworker. I saw how I am here to be the light in other people's darkness with my story and my soul talents.

And I said yes to a whole new journey.

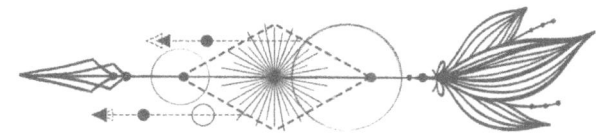

RIDING THE CREATIVE WAVE
OF CHAOS

"A winner is a dreamer who never gave up."
NELSON MANDELA

*B*eing able to take the uncomfortable route to blast your limiting paradigms wide open is a non-negotiable exchange for accessing deep and long-lasting flow. It's literally like being able to stand on the edge of an aeroplane, 15,000 miles up in the air, and jump... without a parachute!

Why would you jump, you may ask yourself?

And the answer is because you WANT to experience the fall.

You might feel like life is calling you right now. More adventure, more exhilaration, more experiences, more opportunities. They all lie in the unknown. The Unknown is the seat of your creative mind. We don't allow ourselves to dance in the unknown because of all the fears we have. Even with the parachute on, we won't take the jump in case the parachute fails. And as I wrote previously, we even fear our success, because we fear we won't be able to handle it. We have to start believing that our own wings will catch us before we smash into a million pieces on the ground.

It's a radical example, but this is the level of trust and delusion you must have to become a powerful Manifestor. Delusion created multiple six figures in my business. The stories I could tell you are INSANE! You couldn't make them up. I had someone who I gave my heart to because she reminded me so much of me and my journey... who I believed so deeply I could help... walk away with thousands and thousands of dollars of free support because I believed her when she told me she would "pay later."

Then there was the million-dollar libel suit when I'd celebrated (anonymously) a new client's desire to overcome PTSD and stated how I did not think PTSD was a life sentence. I had been diagnosed with PTSD after the rape. I had overcome this life sentence. However, this client evidently felt that PTSD was a part of her identity that she felt threatened to let go of it. This is a classic example of the victim consciousness I've talked about in this book. The idea of freedom threatened this lady so much that attached to this libel suit was the confirmation she wouldn't be paying the instalments on the course she had bought. The suit was basically a threat. Let me off these payments, and I'll let you off this libel suit. The libel suit had no foundation though.

Like the guy Aubrey Marcus interviewed in his podcast who described our society like the "Victim Olympics," everyone is fighting to be the biggest victim, and our society is set up to support this. Compensation, libel suits, everyone suing each other. It's easier to give up our power than face the uncomfortable beliefs we have about ourselves, the limiting beliefs that our experiences gave to us. "Powerless" is the core state of most people who haven't begun the journey of their self-healing. Looking outside of themselves for the issues they are manifesting from their victim consciousness, then blaming others when the solutions don't work. Now, I would rather own the responsibility of whatever decision I make in neutrality one hundred times, over continuing to shun responsibility because deep down this satisfies the limiting beliefs I have about myself.

However, how do you wake up when you do not know you are sleeping? If you are not willing to allow yourself to be challenged to uplevel and not able to see obstacles as opportunities, you will always quit at the first uncomfortable hurdle. Like those four ladies who signed up to my course after my Challenge and then pulled out. The reality of the money they had committed was too uncomfortable. They were already deciding they could not pay the instalments they had committed to, based on what they knew about themselves and their world right at that moment. However, the truth was... they couldn't know. Everything can change in a moment.

The challenges we experience are gifted to us, so that we can identify the areas in which we need to grow, so that we can receive the abundance we pray for, the money, the impact, the adventures. Change happens in the unknown. In the unknown, you find yourself manifesting everything you need to GROW into the person who can create what it is you really want. You could say (and I honestly believe) that *the universe doesn't give you what you want until you are ready to receive it. And you must be willing to lose everything you have, to gain everything you want, including the parts of yourself that are holding you back.*

When I finally launched my Mastermind—my "one-stop shop" for women who walk against the grain of convention, who light their own path and shine their own soul spirit through their divine message and mission—where you can get everything, I felt was powerful in stepping up your income and impact, I hired a lady to offer a coaching certification as part of the package. She was the lady I had studied to be a coach through. I valued and respected her so much. So many people have said to me, through my journey, "Wow! I wish I could do what you do!" Having coaching skills can be life changing for you and the people you work with.

However, after a few weeks, I started getting complaints about this lady. She was turning up to sessions late and cancelling. I then received a horrifying message from a client saying she was pretty sure that the lady showed up to the session drunk. I remembered how, when I had been doing my certification with her, she had shared her relationship with alcohol as being challenging. I called her and tried to speak to her about the accusation, but she fought me and denied it. I told her she couldn't stay in my programme. She then asked me to pay the remaining money I owed her. I couldn't believe it. She showed no responsibility. I'd already paid her 50% of the agreement we had made upfront and she hadn't yet exchanged that in services to me.

By this point, I was working with really good lawyers who said she really should give me a refund, but I didn't want to fight her for that. I just wanted to move on and make sure I delivered what I had promised to my clients. That is actually where my own certification was born! In the pure unknown. In sitting in the discomfort of what had happened, having no clue what to do, thanking the Universe for the situation that asked me to uplevel. My creativity switched on, and the idea of the *Quantum Leap Intensive* was born. Now this is a stand-alone programme and is so much more aligned to me and my Soul Goal!

I feel like every challenge I have been gifted as my business has grown has mirrored a part of my own victim consciousness, limiting beliefs, and fears. A little before Benson died, when my youngest daughter had that illness and was in hospital, there was a moment when it seemed serious. They couldn't figure out what was wrong with her. She was completely out of it, and they were talking about doing a lumbar puncture if she didn't improve within 12 hours to check for meningitis and other scary things.

I held her in my arms, and I cried. I realised that if I were to lose her, I would regret the time I had spent in my business and not fully present with her. I would regret the choices I had made to choose clients over time with her, especially considering clients had just walked away without paying. I made a promise to her in the hospital that I would change things, but I didn't keep it. Life just went back to normal when we left the hospital. School runs, the business, and the kids' busy social calendars.

Sometimes it takes an interruption to your "normal" to realise how easy it could be to shake your "normal" up for good. When I lost Benson and dropped into ritual, it was an easy decision because everything inside of me resisted the "normal" that had taken Benson away. The human condition is to wait for "normal" to change. Without something to shatter our paradigm, the feelings related to creating the new habits that step us into the identity that breaks our patterns of "normal" are the more uncomfortable ones. And so, we just keep creating the same reality. Every day!

The resistance we feel doesn't lead us to be believe that it "can be easy."

But the truth is...Your reality can be anything you want it to be. You can have it all, and it can be easy.

However, if you truly want something different to be your "normal"... you must change first! Your entire reality mirrors you. You have to start saying yes, in spite of your uncomfortable feelings and resistance, so you can take different action, and you can make all of this easier by DECIDING how things are going to be. Going back to the very first step of this book and setting your UNLEASHED vision and intention.

Then, you just make it happen. You cannot quit. Whatever you want is already alive in the Quantum Field anyway...

When Benson died, it was like I just let go of the rope I had come so close to hanging myself on. Benson's sacrifice triggered the inner knowing that I could, and that is the true essence of manifestation—your instinctual nature will always know exactly how to respond. You just never give it a chance to respond because your survival reaction kicks in first—the planning, the structuring, the need to control and make sure you feel safe. You might feel relaxed and comfortable this way, but you only have access to what you already know in your survival brain. There is no creativity there and no power to respond.

When you can swap trauma for trust, you will access your inner knowing, tap into far memory, and be able to use the powerful inner perception of your repti.ian brain for powerful creative purposes.

Stepping across from my old business. helping people share their story on social media and mastering the algorithm to my new business doing transformational and intuitive work was exactly like this. I didn't have a plan. Nobody I spoke to could really grasp what I was trying to create, and I just had to be open to learn relentlessly, be fully in the moment, and keep accessing, expressing, and realising the power of my most magical and divine self.

It was literally like riding a creative wave of chaos.

No more planning and strategizing.

Just going with my feelings at every moment.

Letting go and being fully open to new horizons.

When you are stuck in survival mode, you are only focused on what you must do to make the next sale, pay the next bill, and keep yourself safe. Really, you are not fully committed to the goals you say you have, and you are committed to the struggles you have because your focus on them makes you feel safe. You are staying in control, but you are saying no to quantum surprises, the head fuck of Abundance. The Universe will never give you what you think you need, but it will always give you what you actually need to give you what you truly want.

Quantum surprises are where you allow the Universe to show you the fastest route to where you want to go, and you just keep saying yes to whatever adventure gets offered to you along the way. The path will always be the most direct when you are connected to your Source. So, now the question is... How do you create that deep connection?

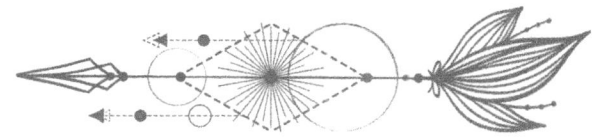

YOUR SOUL CALL TO ADVENTURE

"In reality we know nothing, for truth is in the depths."
DEMOCRITUS

I won't settle for a life that is ordinary. My dad used to call me difficult because of this, and I used to feel all the shame of that burden on them.

I realise now how the dirt I'd felt I couldn't wash off my whole life wasn't my poverty identity at all. It was the shame I felt for being me.

It was why I kept the rape quiet. It felt like someone would tell me it had been my fault. I pushed away friends, relationships, and my family. I was so angry, and I would claim it was never my fault when relationships broke down. I would make the problem about them and something they had done wrong. I blamed countless boyfriends for breaking my heart, but the truth was that my heart was already broken. If you are reading this book, and you were one of my victims, I am sorry. I am so sorry. Ultimately the heaviness in my heart from all the words I hadn't spoken got too heavy, and the discomfort finally became too much. I just had to get the words out in the only way I knew how—to write—and the words became stories, and the stories became this book. And as I dug into my stories, I saw other perspectives, and they began to create new potential in my life.

Victim Consciousness. Even once we have risen from it, we can find ourselves back in it so that the Universe can show us the stories and the fears that cannot come with us into our next growth level.

Remember that:

1. We are programmed to do the things that keep us safe, not fulfilled.
2. Money is the mirror of your self-worth so your ability to receive money is a reflection of how much you BELIEVE you are worthy.
3. Investing in yourself, whether it is time to do your own transformation work or money spent on a mentor to guide you, will multiply your results tenfold.

The real question for most people is when to lose the excuses and simply begin. And what is the first step?

At the end of 2022, I discovered a fraudulent chargeback of around $18K had been made in my stripe account, the payment gateway I use to take payments for clients. The difference between a disputed transaction and chargeback fraud is when the chargeback system is dishonestly manipulated by those seeking to make illicit profit, i.e., a gain that you are not lawfully entitled to obtain. The burden of proof, however, is on the merchant to prove the fraud, and so the money is debited from your stripe account while the dispute process plays out. The crazy thing about the timing of this incident is that the money disappeared as we were leaving for my eight-week trip away to host my first in-person retreat in Tulum, Mexico. And it literally landed back with me the day we were heading home. I had so many learnings from this experience. The money I had to use to cover the stripe debit was the money I'd been saving to cover the trip, which now I know was ridiculous because I earn five-figure months consistently. Why did I feel I needed a safety net? I believe the Universe was inviting me to let go of more old money programming, so I could step into the paradigm I've been asking for.

You'll understand now, after reading this book, that if you hold onto money in the intention of it being a safety net, it says in your energy that there is something you need to be safe from. I do not believe that to be true for me anymore. I'd put off taking this trip for a really long time because I was afraid of taking time out from my business "in case something happened with the business and we ended up struggling financially while we were away." It was when I saw the "untruth" in this limiting belief that I booked the flights. And once again, the Universe gifted me the experience I needed to GROW.

I had to face the discomfort that the safety net that was intended to make me feel comfortable wasn't there. Because I was taking the trip to host my retreat, a bulk of its expenses and expenses around the trip were due in December. When my stripe account was hit with such a big chargeback, it caused a few issues that actually caused my stripe account to be frozen. This meant that all the money that was due to come in from clients and sales during my time away was also frozen. So, I landed exactly where I had been afraid to be… thousands of miles from home, with no money coming in.

In the words of my old Money Coach, "worrying is praying." The energy of what you don't want calls in exactly what you don't want. I'm not going to lie, I buried my head in the sand over Christmas about the invoices that I knew were due, then I realised that this habit came from a very old fear programme I used to run that made me avoid stuff.

I'll never forget cracking six figures in my business and then having my husband walk in the kitchen and ask why we only had six dollars in our personal bank account. I wasn't paying myself because of my fear in spending the money. My fear caused me to avoid looking at my accounts. In this present moment, I made the CHOICE not to let fear take me back to this old fearful identity. I looked at my accounts. I owed $29.7K.

With my safety net gone and payments not coming in, I didn't have $29.7K. I do have a profit hold account though. I'd been following the *Profit First Method* for a while, but had forgotten to act on the bit where you do something with the money on hold. I checked the account, and I was mind blown to see what was in there… $29,288. I mean, of course there was. Later in the trip, a few incidentals also came up in the week of the retreat, and we actually didn't have the money to cover them in the moment either. Then, my phone pinged and I "randomly" received an unexpected affiliate payment.

This is what it means to access your **Miracle Frequency**. The Universe supports you, and synchronicities and miracles come to you. This is the true nature of abundance, there is always enough. And while surrendering to this truth is hard because it challenges everything you have been programmed to believe, **Awakened Wealth** gives you abundant choice because you *trust this truth*. This trust will trigger the Universe to work miracles like you have some magic key that is opening all doors. Awakening the Miracle Frequency that I activated when I dedicated my life to ritual is now at the foundation of everything I do. And Awakened Wealth is now my Movement of Visionaries creating a new world, where we are all more creative, inventive, responsive, and powerful.

This has been my experience since I lost Benson and took my life to ritual. We are divinely held and supported by the Universe, as long as we are connected deeply with our purpose, and I was being gifted the opportunity to let go of the final habits that held the intention in my energy that said I didn't truly believe that. The Universe continued to provide for us the whole trip, and my purpose deepened as we travelled.

A true Shaman must go through 24 ancient rites of passage to develop their genuine shamanic capacities. A big part of these rites is overcoming fear. One of the big fears that was illuminated by the fraud was related to my dad's loss of his business. He lost his business to fraud. I got to see how this isn't my story and how nothing takes away your power in a situation if you can remain emotionally neutral.

It's the holding on, attaching and reacting from the place of your limiting beliefs that is the "decider" of your fate. Holding onto a certain belief and/or attaching to a certain outcome. Digging into the reasons you might be doing either of these things will be the most liberating journey of your life. You get to let go. You get to heal. And you get to forgive.

Multiple times, through this experience, I have held the person who raised this fraudulent claim in a healing white light. I have seen her limiting stories and her pain. I have forgiven her and sent her healing. This is the beauty of "challenges," you get to grow through them and expand, and you get to see the beliefs that are keeping you stuck and small. Whatever your challenge, situation or experience is, you can allow and receive the growth from it with curiosity and openness or you can resist and react and fight and miss the opportunity to grow. For me to serve my deep purpose, another part of my identity from the past still needed to "die."

I felt so connected to Spirit during my eight-week trip around the retreat. In Mexico, I could feel the all-encompassing Spirit in everything. I also felt this strong, metaphysical, unified connection to every Visionary Light Leader working for the good of the planet and was drawn to providing even more support to them. The birds talked to me, animals greeted me everywhere I went, and my super sensory capacity was off the charts. I noticed every little sound and movement that nature brought in gratitude. I felt aligned. My limiting beliefs about the true nature of abundance couldn't come forward with me into a multi-million-dollar empire.

I invite you to ask yourself right now before I connect you to say yes to your own soul's call to adventure... What if whatever experience you are in right now that feels challenging is happening exactly BECAUSE it's bringing you the gift of what you need to learn? The ability to allow and receive is what awakens your Miracle Frequency.

My Miracle Frequency felt even stronger. Right on the edge of a new year, with a new opportunity to build my business even bigger, I had deep new learnings for my new level of business. Coupled with my experience in Mexico, I also felt even more passionate about standing for what is sacred and trusting ancient wisdom. From within I trusted I was okay. At not one single point did I look externally for validation of that. I trusted all the way through that in whatever way I would rise—like the phoenix—and bring even more value to the world. I consistently allowed and received divine guidance and took timely action.

I was like the girl who made the fraudulent claim once. When I lost my job in Manchester, I blamed the company and claimed unfair dismissal. I'm not saying the claim was fraudulent, but I took advantage of a system to avoid taking responsibility for myself. Maybe the fraudulent chargeback was my karma! I was the common factor in all the situations in my life up to that point that had led me right there—misaligned and miserable—I never made myself the hero of my story but I always made myself the victim. In the unfair dismissal, I pinned ALL my hopes of bouncing back in life from the depression I was in on winning that claim. I felt entitled, and I was so attached to the outcome that my life froze in time for many, many months.

This experience was so different. Throughout the whole thing, I refused to become the block in my energetic currency of money, impact, growth or anything else as a reaction to the circumstances I was in. I practised what I preach. I trusted the whole situation was happening for me, not to me, and I allowed myself to see the stories and the fears that couldn't come with me into my UNLEASHED vision of myself and my world. What I know for sure is that the more we open up this energetic channel of abundance, the more value we pour into the world. And the more value we pour, the more we help the world and those we love. Our unique journeys touch others and inspire others to heal. The world needs this right now. So, what do you truly want? How do you light your Soul Fire? You can have it all, and it can be easy. The "MAGIC KEY" is to not be attached to the outcomes you seek.

You find this detachment in the moment. And in this detachment, you awaken your Miracle Frequency. If you are open, you are going to take your life to ritual now, just like I did, using my 7x7 Method. As you now know—action, creation, and attraction—come from how you feel. The 7x7 Method helps you practise inner stillness in the simplest and most self-nourishing way, so you can find the inner peace I did as I inhaled and lifted my mind out of my body and realised that I was none of my feelings. This is where I found "the space." In the space, you can see the sacred in all things, and if you need to, look at things from another perspective.

You may be thinking, "What is different about your method compared to other meditation tools?"

I created the 7x7 Method in an app with 7 neurosomatic rituals that you can do in just 7 minutes to synchronise your heart and mind and connect to your trust, truth, and divine assistance 7 times a day. I made this app in a way that will help you move away from your excuses towards alignment with your Soul's true goal. If your Soul is calling you to adventure right now, within the app you will have access to support from me and access to a beautiful community of others on the same journey as you. And the best news is... it's all free.

PRACTICAL INTEGRATION

The 7x7 Method WORKS. I have had clients manifest 30-40K months using it!

Go to Google Play or iTunes and download the *"Awakened Wealth"* App. Sign up to the app for free then watch the Welcome Video! Some people like to ease their way into using the Method. The utopia is to take 7 pauses a day (these can include your morning and evening ritual), pick a method from the app in each pause and drop into ritual. You may find you prefer some methods over others. It doesn't matter which ones you use; however, I do recommend you use the Reduced Breathing and Manifestation Breathing daily. If you want a longer ritual, you can put methods together. Like yoga then breathing or breathing then meditation. The rituals use brainwave entrainment music from my mentor, Niraj Naik. It is beautiful to open and close sacred space when you do the rituals. You can do this by lighting a candle, saying a prayer, or even just by feeling gratitude. The goal is to create neutrality emotionally in each ritual and then raise your vibration. You will start to notice how, as you drop into ritual every day, you begin to live in more love and forgiveness, see new perspectives, and let go of bitterness and regrets. You will also feel more connected to your unique story and message, meaning you can lead with more brand authority, confidence, and authenticity, and stop breaking the promises you make to yourself by giving your power away to the busyness of life and misplaced loyalties.

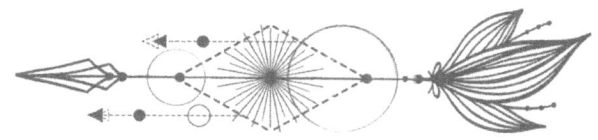

YOUR TREE – YOUR SYMBOL OF GROWTH

"Root Girl sits shivering, unclear and naked, at the base of the tree of the Self. She is unloved, unwanted, and shunned… Could this urchin be the one part of you that reintegration can lead you to wholeness and true purpose? This is a part of you, the embodiment of a deeply flawed perception of your failures, manifesting as guilt and shame… If you would only look into the Root Girl's eyes and see the beauty and the unmet need, your unmet needs, you would realise that this part of you asks for your compassion and understanding. This part of you was born when you were wounded and were conditioned to believe you're not whole, that your expression of self is somehow too much or too little. You may have even inherited the creature from your ancestors. However, it was this child self who came to be curled up at the roots of your sacred tree self. It's time to welcome her into your heart. When you do, everything you've been searching for becomes illuminated, and your path lights

> up with renewed purpose. When you come
> to love Root Girl and claim her as your own,
> accepting her as your own, accepting her and
> your humanity, she is transformed, just as you
> are. Then, all manner of magic begins to arrive
> in abundant form."
> ~ ALBERTO VILLOLDO, THE SHAMAN'S DREAM
> ORACLE

When I first began writing this book, I thought that my story, this story, was about a girl who had experienced a rape that stopped the wheels turning on her life. It has evolved into so much more. It is now a story about a girl who, ever since she was young, has been fighting to prove that everything is possible. No adversity is so great that we cannot overcome it with a fresh perspective that leads to expansion. And now I understand how we don't have to fight at all.

While I was in Mexico, Spirit brought a powerful message to me. It challenged my paradigms after years of believing we have to fight to conserve forest fragments. The message said that everything is okay. I was assured that nature has its own "plan" and that humans are interfering both with their action to conserve the forests and their action to destroy it. A few weeks before receiving that message, I had received a similar one about extinction. The message shared that extinction is completely natural. Species will always come and go (including humans) and that again, our "interference" comes from a place of scarcity instead of abundance. We can do things differently. I was invited to approach things differently.

I was sure, after these messages, that my calling as the *Millionaire Sha'Woman* is to bring the peace I have brought to my own "inner being" to more people through this book and the Awakened Wealth app and community, so that more people will bring more kindness to the land. I no longer feel like I am here to fix the impossible so that I can resolve the hopelessness I felt growing up when I watched my mum succumb to the mental illness that had its claws into her. I am no longer trying to prove my worth where I had not earned it growing up. My action is from a place of abundance and love. I am here to raise the frequency of the planet and lead a Movement of other Light Leaders who are also ready to bring positive change to the world by transforming themselves from the inside out.

When I was part of *Play to Win*, the Reality Show, in 2019, the host talked about how it's okay to help people just because it feels good. For so long, I had tried to find a reason to care so much, to somehow justify it, but in hearing his words, I came full circle. It is simply because it feels good. And that is a good thing! LOVE is the highest level of vibrational energy. We all need more unconditional love, of ourselves and of others. When we heal the parts of ourselves that are wounded, we are able to find this unconditional love, so that it activates our abundance within, which mirrors in the abundance we get around us as well.

If you are ready to heal and love every part of yourself, you can unleash the Millionaire that is already within, and make millions by impacting millions! Make sure you have taken the step in the previous chapter. I am waiting to support you to have radical expression of your Soul Goal and move your business forward with purpose. As I wrote in the chapter, "Armours," moving forward is "like stepping through the eye of a needle, where there is no space for your limiting beliefs and stories to come with you." You must become so focused on your

UNLEASHED vision, that it becomes easy to remove anything that isn't aligned, and your vibration begins to remove
everything that isn't for you. You must be ready to see how
your life begins to fall apart from the positive perspective of
how it is actually aligning for you, so that you get everything
you want and you get it easily. The ease comes in your agreement to let go and allow something meaningful and new to
manifest for you. And remember this arrives in the complete
unknown. All you have to "know" is your true desires, your
deepest Soul Goal, and what is true to you.

Through this book, I do still hope to lend a voice to the plight
of the Atlantic Rainforest in Brazil and plant 100,000 trees,
but my perspective on this mission is different. I no longer
believe in the limiting paradigm that things are scarce, and
so this book is not my expression of trying to hold onto what
is left or try to control the forest's regrowth. It is my expression of the belief that the life of the forest is still thriving and
abundant and by reading this book and making the changes
that align you to your own soul goal, there will be a powerful
ripple effect that brings harmony back to nature. It is impossible to raise your frequency and not bring more love and kindness back to your everyday actions in life. And every time you
make a different decision, the earth's pulse will beat through
the roots of your tree and it will flourish and grow. Its growth
will be the mirror of your growth. Your flourishing tree will be
the symbol of your Abundance.

The Atlantic Rainforest is one of the most endangered ecosystems of the world. Europeans began burning trees in the
Atlantic to make way for settlements and agriculture in the
16th century. What once blanketed 1.3 million square kilo-
metres and was ranked as one of the world's largest tropical
forests, had shrunk to 8% of its former size by 1973, when protective laws were put in place. Around 7% is left of it today.

Maybe you have never heard about the Atlantic Rainforest, but you have likely seen this forest in pictures or movies. It's the landscape in Brazil's most famous image, the one of the Christ the Redeemer statue in Rio de Janeiro.

The forest follows the Atlantic coastline from the easternmost part of Brazil to the southern border and beyond, into Paraguay. It encompasses some of the largest cities in Brazil, such as São Paulo and Rio, and is home to more than 145 million people. Its biodiversity is as impressive as the Amazon's and its plight is so much more critical. While the Amazon has lost 19% of its original tree cover, the Atlantic Forest has lost more than 90%, and there are forest fragments just like it all over the world.

After hundreds of years of deforestation and predatory exploration for natural resources all over the world, it is time to recognize all forest fragments as the important ecosystems they are. When I was in Tulum, Mexico, I initially struggled to feel the "constraints" of nature. Tulum doesn't feel deforested, it feels like a jungle that has been built on top of, and I was able to feel the jungle's life pulling through the bricks and buildings. That is the true abundance of nature; it will always be more powerful than us.

I am choosing to support Iracambi with my business because they are pioneers of a model that is duplicatable in other areas of forest degradation across the world. The Atlantic Forest also provides one of the most important opportunities for landscape restoration in the world. Restoring the degraded land with native plants would combat climate change, safeguard exceptional biodiversity, and boost Brazil's rural economy. Iracambi has been working since the year 2000 to make the conservation of the Atlantic Rainforest more attractive than its destruction. They are encouraging people to bring more kindness to the land. Since 2000, they have been purchasing land from locals in the buffer zone of the Serra do Brigadeiro State Park in the mountains of South Eastern Brazil to reforest. They engage in managing natural resources, developing sustainable communities, and researching ecosystems. Iracambi is not just a non-governmental organisation, it's a community of people across the world with the same objective. You cannot help but feel hope when you see the work that Iracambi does, and in 2022, they also adopted the mission to help people "Go Farther and Dream Higher" with thriving communities in their focus living in a thriving landscape.

Iracambi's mission aligns so beautifully with my own. Taking a forest that is barely surviving to thriving and giving hope to others who are in situations that feel impossible to overcome.

My gift to you and Iracambi for purchasing this book is a tree that will be planted in the Brazilian Atlantic. I invite you see it as your symbol of growth, just as the rebirth of the forest in Brazil will be a global symbol of hope. Nothing is impossible to overcome! As a forest that would seem like it is impossible to save, with just a tiny 7% of it left, is brought back from the brink of extinction, the dreams of women all over the world will be reignited. Their focus will shift from their troubles in life to creating and manifesting. And in their hearts, they will believe, just like I do, with their Miracle Frequency Awakened, and their desires assured by divine force, that it truly is EASIER THAN YOU THINK TO HAVE IT ALL.

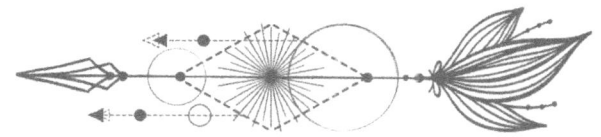

ACKNOWLEDGMENTS

To all people who helped me to get this book off the ground in the first place. It's crazy now to think that I first had to ask for financial help to get started with the publishing process. It has taken quite a journey, as have I. I hope it feels amazing to finally get this book in your hands after so many years.

To my 3 beautiful children and the love of my life that co-created you. Thank you all for being with me on this journey of writing this book. You guys have always been and always will be my biggest reason to keep deepening this journey into my soma and to keep dropping under my ego, so we can live into our life together in ever growing freedom, peace and love. I know you three smallbies are going to pip this effort to make a difference to the world. You all hold the world inside of you and I love you all so much.

To the Williamsons. You took me under your wing and have each inspired me and supported me in different and beautiful ways. I'll always be forever grateful and feel so blessed to be part of your family!

Mum and Dad. I couldn't have written this book without our story. I hope it is as healing for you to read it as it was for me to write it. I want you to know, you can let go too. You can let go of any part of you that feels broken, shameful or "faulty" because it's not. I know you are tired. You can rest now, in truth and in trust. The truth is that love in its purest essence is unconditional and you can trust through "that lens"... the world is so beautiful. You are beautiful. I love you both so much.

Lil and the GWN Publishing Team. Holy moly guys... we did it. Lil, thank you so much for your belief in me. There has not been one moment where I haven't felt supported. Thank you for making me excited again about bringing this book to the world!

ABOUT THE AUTHOR

CLARE WILLIAMSON is a Transformational Business Coach, Mum Of 3, Best-Selling Author, Speaker and Shaman. She was born in Britain, but calls New Zealand home after moving there in 2011. Clare has 4 passions - her kids, helping people, saving rainforests and travelling. Her biggest achievement to date has been finding a way to knit those passions together, through her Coaching Business, which helps other Visionary Light Leaders to unleash their soul's goal from the limits of their mind, so they can live a life of abundant choice and maximum impact.

www.ingramcontent.com/pod-product-compliance
Lightning Source LLC
Chambersburg PA
CBHW051612120626
46551CB00014B/1759